HUMANITY
AGAINST ITSELF

HUMANITY
AGAINST ITSELF

The Retreat from Reason

BENJAMIN KOVITZ, MD

Prometheus Books

59 John Glenn Drive
Amherst, New York 14228–2119

Published 2008 by Prometheus Books

Inquiries should be addressed to
Prometheus Books
59 John Glenn Drive
Amherst, New York 14228–2119
VOICE: 716–691–0133, ext. 210
FAX: 716–691–0137
WWW.PROMETHEUSBOOKS.COM

12 11 10 09 08   5 4 3 2 1

Library of Congress Cataloging-in-Publication Data pending

Kovitz, Benjamin, 1913–
    Humanity against itself : the retreat from reason / Benjamin Kovitz.
        p. cm.
    Includes bibliographical references.
    ISBN 978–1–59102–573–3 (alk. paper)
    1. Psychology—Philosophy. 2. Religion and science. I. Title.
    [DNLM: Psychological Theory. 2. Psychoanalytic Theory. 3. Religion and Science. BF 38 K88h 2008]

BF38K88h 2008
150.19'5—dc22

                                                            2008004519

Printed in the United States of America on acid-free paper

To Miriam

CONTENTS

INTRODUCTION

The human species is a novel but unsuccessful experiment. Its failings apparently reflect the long and complex evolution of the human brain. The theory of a triune brain posits the successive development over time of three distinct levels of brain function. The oldest and most primitive level is the reptilian brain, dedicated to instinct and control of the vital organs. The limbic brain, which first appeared in early mammals, records memories and generates emotions. The neocortex of the cerebral hemisphere developed much later, enabling human primates to communicate through language and to engage in rational thought. Our superior mental competence is nevertheless hampered by the imperfect coordination of these three components, which sometimes work at cross-purposes. Emotions often arise with urgent intensity, while the exercise of reason needs patient cultivation if we are to achieve a civilized existence.

The human race, which flatters itself with the scientific name of *Homo sapiens* (intelligent man), is a remarkable species of primate but has had little success in understanding its own nature. We tend to overestimate our powers and underestimate our limitations. The world fascinates us, but we constantly evade what we find disturbing, especially the full truth about ourselves. We are deeply divided between conflicting motives we can neither reconcile nor relinquish. Most notably, consideration for others can interfere with what we feel we owe to ourselves. Unable to unravel these inner contradictions, we often ignore what we cannot resolve. We are also prone to errors that are later too embarrassing to admit. To evade responsibility for such errors, we blame our adversaries or the vagaries of nature, even though we created these difficulties for ourselves. The gap between what we do and what we say, to ourselves and to others, shows how deeply we resist reason and self-discipline.

Disharmony has consistently marked not only the life of the individual but the state of the world. Civilization, which might have been a supreme achievement, is on the verge of turning into a supreme disaster. There is no limit to the questions that divide us. Should our first priority be power or peace? Must we resign ourselves to our senseless rivalries? Can we honor the intrinsic worth of every person, or must we despise those who fail to meet our prescribed standards? Are we to believe in a God? And if so, what kind of God? If we cannot resolve even the first of these dilemmas, let alone the rest, our future is precarious.

It should disturb us more than it does to acknowledge the gulf between what we are and what we could be. Yet recognizing the gravity of the issues is merely a beginning. The entrenched realities of our existence will not change of their own accord. Then what can we do, engulfed as we are in a confusing world? Hindsight can be unreliable, but foresight is even more unreliable. Our failings still do not destroy the stubborn conviction that we are worth saving. With little to guide us but our hope and such intelligence as we command, we can at least take certain steps that hold promise of a more endurable future.

We first need to submit our own assumptions, motives and behavior to a scrupulous and thorough reexamination. This is our primary challenge. Complete honesty with ourselves will enable us to treat our neighbors and even our adversaries with greater tact and understanding. Respect for human differences is essential, because until we know on exactly what grounds others base their positions, we are unprepared to negotiate the peaceful coexistence to which reasonable minds aspire.

Humanity has always resisted confronting the formidable task of creating a true civilization. Yet our future as a viable species depends on how we deal with an existential crisis of our own making, one for which we can expect no one else to take responsibility. As the Talmud reminds us:

> It is not your duty to complete the work, but neither are you free to desist from it.
>
> Mishnah, Pirkei Avot 2.21 (Sayings of the Fathers)

PART ONE

HUMAN NATURE

W hat is human nature? When José Ortega y Gasset wrote, "Man has no 'nature'; he has history," he was telling us not that we lack innate potentialities, but that we define ourselves in the course of developing them. Becoming human is a process of self-creation. Although social beings need to maintain a consistent identity, there is no way they can avoid changing as they grow. In some respects, people of the present day are copies of our ancestors; in other respects, it is no longer possible to think or behave as our ancestors did. We therefore proceed to describe contemporary personality from three perspectives: *motivation, emotion*, and *psyche* (a term more precise than *mind*).

MOTIVATION

In his reflective book *Civilization and its Discontents* (*Das Unbehagen in der Kultur*), Sigmund Freud made these comments about human motivation:

> Die individuelle entwicklung erscheint uns als ein Produkt der Inter-
> ferenz zweier Strebungen, des Strebens nach Glück, das wir
> gewöhnlich "egoistisch," und des Strebens nach Vereinigung mit
> dem anderen in der Gemeinschaft, das wir "altruistisch" heissen.
> Beide Bezeichnungen gehen nicht viel über die Oberfläche hinaus.

Translation by Joan Riviere:

> Individual development seems to be a product of two trends, the
> striving for happiness, generally called 'egoistic,' and the impulse
> toward merging with others in the community, which we call 'altru-
> istic.' Neither of these descriptions goes far beneath the surface.

Since Freud dismissed these *Strebungen* (tendencies) as superficial, he
ascribed behavior to two drives that parallel the constructive and
destructive forces of nature. The drive for greater unities he called
Eros (Love); the drive to undo unity and even reduce life to an inor-
ganic state, he called Thanatos (Death). While admitting these were
theoretical constructs, he considered them fundamental and was
pleased to find a precursor in the pre-Socratic philosopher Empedocles
(died about 430 BCE), who identified Love and Strife as the prime
movers of the universe.

Not all psychoanalysts follow Freud. The "object relations" analysts see social interaction as primary. There are also theorists who
believe that although grounds exist for both "drive" and "relational"
models, their grounds are too different to reconcile. But if a choice
between the two cannot be decided empirically, we are dealing with
philosophy rather than science. The dispute is in any case of little
merit. Since organic motives and interpersonal relations are inseparable, why argue about which comes first? Personal interaction and
organic drive are instinctively fused, for example, in the experience of
genuine sexual love.

Freud saw that egoism and altruism have diverse implications. In
the passage quoted earlier, he describes their relation as one of *Inter-
ferenz* (interference), a word the translator omitted. Egoism puts one-

self first, but if this were our only motive, it would deny others the right to pursue their own aims. Even altruism, a basic expression of empathy, diminishes with emotional distance like a law of inverse squares. The pain of someone known who arouses our concern matters more than the suffering of unknown thousands; indifference toward the stranger is commonplace. At ideal moments, however, egoism and altruism are transcended in the total submission to divine will that Dante described in the line:

> *In la sua volontade è nostra pace.*
> In His will is our peace.
> *Paradiso*, canto 3.85

That achievement is rare, for neither inner nor outer disharmony is easy to overcome. We therefore need to discover what we are best meant to do with our lives, as Keats was inspired to write poetry, Caesar to acquire power, and Newton to understand the cosmos. The pursuit of our goals is nevertheless limited not only by inner contradiction but by the forces of a world not subject to our will. Every drive for fulfillment must adapt to a larger reality, for whatever it may be, reality has the last word. Even if it is a dream, it is a dream we cannot summon or dispel at will.

> Men must endure
> Their going hence, even as their coming hither:
> Ripeness is all.
> Shakespeare, *King Lear*

Egoism and altruism, like the Freudian drives, are more descriptive than explanatory. In his *Foundations for a Science of Personality,* Andras Angyal introduced a different pair of motives: the "trend to autonomy," which he defined as acting in accord with one's own nature, and the "trend to homonymy," which he defined as acting in accord with the requirements of one's culture or society. When the two trends work together, as they often do, they enhance both personal success and communal order. Angyal's concepts have also been recognized under other names. Alfred Adler, for instance, realized that Nietzsche's "will to power" needed to be balanced by "social interest." Several centuries earlier, Spinoza had already defined autonomy as the endeavor of everything to persist in its own being (*Ethics* 3, proposition 6).

In proposing his pair of coordinated motives, Angyal was aware that everything alive strives to exert whatever power it commands, yet no living thing is wholly self-sufficient. Since creatures necessarily differ in their needs and goals, interaction with the world involves individual purposes and choices. Behaviorists have tried to dispense with these concepts in their futile pursuit of a purely objective approach. B. F. Skinner, for instance, maintained that what he called "objective contingencies of reinforcement" should replace the subjective term *purpose*. But by engaging in such activities as writing, publishing, and defending his theories, Skinner was certainly acting with purpose.

Purpose is intention with a specific goal. We call it *will* when it is firm and unswerving, but like many psychological terms, *will* has other connotations. Whereas *will* implies a determined effort to bring about a particular end, *willpower* is a dubious notion that serves mainly for rationalizing or sermonizing. Rudolf Dreikurs, an Adlerian therapist, makes the point:

> Willpower is a fiction. It doesn't exist, because it could only exist if there were something like a lack of willpower with which it could be contrasted. But there is never any lack of willpower, since everybody does only what he intends to do. Not to will is just as impossible as not to choose. When I say I lack the willpower to make myself do something, I am in fact saying that my will is not to do it.
> "The Adlerian Approach to Psychodynamics"

Boasts of willpower are actually attempts to support self-esteem; pleas of inadequate willpower are excuses for inaction or failure. I may say that I surrendered my wallet to a robber against my will, but the fact is that I willed that surrender to protect myself from a worse outcome.

Every action reflects all the motives that a situation evokes, whether the actor is fully aware of them or not. What I experience as a state of indecision may actually be an unadmitted act of will, designed to force someone else to make a decision for which I would rather not be responsible.

Purpose is central to life. The one-celled amoeba and the human being are alike in showing preferences and moving toward their natural goals. Everything alive also exhibits a remarkable capacity to vary its routes toward its chosen goals in the face of altered conditions (thereby demonstrating teleology as an explanatory principle).

The word *motive* does not discriminate between intention, emotion, and goal as aspects of behavior. These terms therefore need to be more fully defined. An intention is a decision to take action toward a specific goal. A goal is an end-state that one endeavors to reach or bring about. Striving for a goal and the emotion that accompanies that striving are distinguishable in thought but inseparable in action. Emotion is a psychophysiological state that reports the *quality* of our experience, revealing the success, difficulty, or failure of our endeavors to achieve our goals. The words *motive* and *emotion* both come from the Latin for "motion" or "movement." Our motives "move" us to action. When we are strongly affected by an experience, we say that we are "moved." Motive, action, and emotion occur in a natural combination, no matter how well we try to conceal or deny any of the three, as we do when we try to deceive others or ourselves. We all conceal our motives whenever there is any risk of embarrassment by exposure or misjudgment.

EMOTION

All emotion involves bodily processes, but these are not always felt or understood at a conscious level. Even if we are unaware of such physiological processes as the secretion of stress hormones, we need to experience the conscious emotions if we are to appreciate the full import of a life situation. Our emotions are always expressed by some physical reaction. We smile, we frown, we grimace, we raise our eyebrows, we shrug our shoulders. In laughter, in tears, in losing our temper, emotions are vented with dramatic force.

Laughter expresses a surprised relief from an unnecessary concern. Tears flow as one experiences a painful ordeal or receives unexpected appreciation. Feelings of elation signify success and satisfaction. Feelings of dejection or depression accompany failure or regret. Fear marks the need to escape danger, whereas anger expresses the urge to overcome danger. Anger may also mask a latent doubt about one's right or power to control a situation. Shame reveals that an action has earned not only regret but self-contempt. A feeling of guilt discloses that punishment or reparation is due for one's behavior. Unhappiness about misfortune for which one was not responsible differs clinically from the pathological depression based on guilt-laden resentment toward oneself and others. There are also more complex emotional states, such as admiration, contempt, compassion, or vengefulness. Various conflicting emotions can coexist without annulling each other. Anxiety is a special case of fear that obscures unadmitted motives one can neither justify nor relinquish. (A later chapter will explore anxiety in greater depth.)

Unusual emotional reactions can easily be misjudged. An observer who calls an expression of feeling "inappropriate" has not really understood it. A schizophrenic patient, for instance, may emit an odd laugh while verbalizing anger or fear, but this so-called "splitting," or apparent inconsistency between the words and the feelings, expresses his defensive state of concurrent anger, anxiety, and resignation.

The topic of love presents special complexities. Love is not only an emotion or a motive or a form of behavior; it is all these together. Few words in the English language are so beguiling and so deceptive as *love*. English demands too much of this monosyllable; classical Greek needed four words for different kinds of love. What love means in actual life is learned only through experience. It can include not only the fulfillment of our existence but the pain that sooner or later comes with caring for others. There is no escape from the sorrow life brings when those whom we love or value ultimately suffer, abandon us, or die.

While the love that makes us human includes sex as a necessary part of life, sexuality is not only enjoyed but transcended in conditions of sincere intimacy and family closeness. Sexual love varies with the age and experience of the lovers, from the youthful transport of *Romeo and Juliet* to the fulfillment that a couple achieves through years of mutual caring and trust. It is a serious error, however, to confuse sexual desire with love. The immature adolescent, biologically propelled into sex and stimulated by fantasies, readily idealizes a member of the opposite sex and calls it love. If people are not yet capable of mature love, they often engage in physical sex as a substitute. But sexual titillation unaccompanied by love becomes boring, and further conquests are needed to keep up the excitement, as many discover in time.

What draws us to a particular person comes from a deep and intuitive source. The more mature we are, the more trustworthy our intuition. The lower our self-esteem, the more easily we are misled. Insecure people cannot believe that a desirable partner would accept them. The mistaken choices that often follow undermine self-esteem even further. On the other hand, couples who choose each other on the strength of their compatibility and commitment have a favorable outlook, whatever their other differences. Major differences nevertheless demand mutual respect. The inevitable tensions of intimate living cannot always be foreseen, and it matters greatly how they are handled. The eccentric but insightful William Blake reminded us long ago:

> Mutual forgiveness of each vice,
> Such are the gates of paradise.
> *For the Sexes: The Gates of Paradise*

Harry Stack Sullivan spelled out a definition of *love* with his characteristically extreme precision: "When the satisfaction or the security of another person becomes as significant to one as is one's own satisfaction or security, then the state of love exists. So far as I know, under no other circumstances is a state of love present, regardless of the popular usage of the word" (*Conceptions of Modern Psychiatry*).

Love and desire are different forms of attachment and need to be clearly distinguished. Ortega y Gasset pointed out that desire wants to possess and control, to subordinate the object of desire to one's own needs. Love, on the other hand, affirms its object and experiences self-transcendence through identification with the beloved.

What love means in a particular case can never be taken for granted. Some people say they are "in love" because they were taught it is something everyone should feel. People whose rearing was love-less say the word without ever living the reality. Assertions of love can mask ambivalence that is unadmitted or unrecognized. When unsupported by action, such assertions ultimately ensure disillusion, regret, and recrimination. Protestations of love sometimes serve to camouflage loveless courtships, whose real motives may be escape, dependency, domination, social or financial advantage, or even vanity. Insecure people who sell their souls for "love" at any price usually disregard the warnings that are almost always present in such situations. The supposed security of a submissive dependency soon loses its value when nothing is gained in return. Many a depressed or suicidal woman discovers too late that she has bargained away her fulfillment. It is surprisingly common for a psychiatrist to hear a patient affirm "love" for a cruel and untrustworthy partner. Those whom disappointment drives to suicide or even murder are victims not of love but of tragic self-deception.

Jealousy is a pathological distrust of the fidelity of one's sexual partner. In this state, the preoccupation with love is another self-deceiving mask for one's insecurity. It is a state in which the distinction between love and sex becomes clear only too late in the game. Envy is aroused by a lack of what another enjoys, while jealousy is the specific pain of losing out to a rival in "love." Jealousy is the antithesis of love, for it masks an inability to love or feel worthy of love. Shakespeare provides a dramatic illustration. After killing Desdemona,

Othello speaks of himself as one who loved "not wisely but too well." But he is still deceiving himself. The pain of rejection raises his sense of personal failure to a pitch that is relieved only by an act of murder. So-called lovers who kill because of rejection never *loved* the person they killed; they *needed* that relationship to conceal their own lack of self-worth. What really matters in such jealousy is not the fate of the victim but the humiliation of defeat by a rival.

MIND, PSYCHE, AND SELF

Adapting to the world involves the interplay of two systems, the *psyche* and the *self*. The psyche is the superordinate system; the self is subordinate, but it exercises a significant degree of independence. Inseparable yet distinguishable in function, at times these two systems find themselves at odds. Since each plays a necessary role in the process of adaptation, it is important to see how the two are related and how they become incongruent.

The role of the psyche is fundamental. Originally the word *psyche* meant "breath," but for obvious reasons it soon came to mean "life." The ancient Greeks originally distinguished the life (psyche) from the body (soma), but in time *psyche* acquired a still deeper meaning: the inner life of the mind. In its current scientific use, it has come to mean the capability of an organism to act as a unitary whole, or in more concrete terms, the ability of a living creature to have goals, make choices, experience meanings, and feel emotions. Although capable of consciousness, the psyche is also continually active outside of awareness.

But if the psyche is in some sense a whole, how does a separate self come to operate within it? The answer is that although the psyche's overall goal is integration, its complex and divergent functions prevent it from achieving complete unity. It has accordingly developed the *self* as a subsystem primarily concerned with maintaining an acceptable social image. That image serves to conceal our private reality, at times even from ourselves. As a result of this dual system, we know something of what we are, but we never know all that we are. Like the physical body, the psyche and the self grow but preserve their distinctive identities while undergoing continual change. The self as understood here originates in the response of the developing psyche to appraisal by others. This concept of the self is not accepted by everyone, and other ways of conceiving a self at least deserve mention.

Some thinkers doubt the reality of such an entity because it is deduced rather than observed. For the philosopher Alasdair MacIntyre, the self is the subject—the coauthor with its world—of the unique story that it lives. In the course of living that story, one generates a self and gives it meaning. But this view does not distinguish the self from the psyche. Psychoanalysts were slow to adopt the concept of a self because Freud used the word *Ich* (German "I") to stand for both what we here call the *self* and what his English translators latinized as the *ego*. When later analysts defined the self as one's self-representation in the ego, they gave little attention to its defensive function. Carl Gustav Jung, the Swiss psychiatrist who broke with Freud, conceived the self quite differently, as an archetype or innate pattern that maintains the unity of the psyche. A more recent psychoanalyst, Heinz Kohut, preferred to see the self as a psychological process dedicated to the goal of becoming what one needs to be. The essential function of a self was identified by the social psychologist George Herbert Mead as the role that enables one to function as a member of society. Harry Stack Sullivan elaborated Mead's concept into a "self-dynamism" primarily dedicated to maintaining self-esteem. Mead and Sullivan both emphasized psychological defense and adaptation as primary functions of the self, whereas Kohut underscored integration and fulfillment. Karen Horney gave equal weight to both defense and fulfillment, distinguishing an "actual self" (how one actually lives), an "idealized self" (a compensatory self-image designed to avoid anxiety), and a "real self" (the optimal realization of one's potential). Her concept of a "real self" recalls the seminal essay by José Ortega y Gasset, "In Search of Goethe from Within," which distinguishes an unplanned mode of existence from how one's entelechy or "unique potential" would have one live. Such an entelechy, implicit yet real, is present in the psyche from birth, like an embryo in the womb, but comes to fruition only when acknowledged and nurtured. The realization of our latent entelechy then becomes the ultimate criterion by which we measure the value of our existence.

How does one judge the self? As the term is used here, its primary purpose is to maintain self-esteem. In taking on this task, the self is bound at times to encounter problems that are beyond its power to resolve. This failure usually occurs when personalities that are torn between acceptable and unacceptable motives demonstrate their loss of integrity by developing some type of mental disorder. At such times, an overdefensive self will do whatever it can to keep pertinent but disturbing aspects of reality from entering awareness.

In its depth and range, the unobtrusive power of the self often goes unrecognized. It underlies our preoccupation with how we look, how we behave, and how we dress. It leads us to conceal or disown socially unacceptable aspects of our own reality. Thanks to the self, we learn from an early age to be untruthful not only to others but, whenever necessary, to ourselves. An exaggerated self-image promotes inordinate competition and conflict. As a result, we live on guard much of the time, unable to enjoy the freedom to be what we naturally are.

The adult sense of self is a gradual and continuous development, yet an inchoate experience of one's identity must exist from the start. One cannot expect the infant to practice conscious self-analysis; it has to begin by instinctively accepting itself as it is. This natural self-acceptance is present in all life. Even Cicero remarked long ago, "love of self is inherent in every species" (*De Finibus* 4). Such intuitive freedom from self-consciousness is lost as soon as a defensive self makes the risk of any disapproval its overriding concern.

Although *mind* and *psyche* are comparable terms, the latter is more precise. Both terms imply the unity that consciousness confers on such activities as perceiving, feeling, thinking, knowing, and willing. *Mind* and *consciousness* are therefore often treated as one and the same, but they need to be distinguished, because *mind* includes much that is temporarily or permanently unconscious. The content of awareness changes continually, marked not only by frequent discontinuities but by self-imposed or externally imposed limitations. Consciousness is thus a surface; mind is the depth over which that surface plays. Consciousness focuses primarily on what needs attention at the moment, whereas the psyche as a whole includes far more, some of it available to consciousness (the Freudian preconscious) and some of it denied awareness (the Freudian unconscious). Dream life reaches consciousness in obscure fragments, although it may well go on as a subliminal process parallel to waking awareness and in touch with matters that elude waking life.

The thinking mind has always been a mystery to itself. We are not only conscious but *aware* that we are conscious, whereas inanimate things apparently are not. But our understanding of consciousness runs into difficulty when we try to discriminate between mind and body. Where is consciousness located? There is no way to get outside of our conscious field in order to observe it as we observe an external object. Consciousness pictures our world but is itself unpicturable. Consciousness and brain must be closely related, yet we cannot study consciousness under the microscope as we do a nerve cell. Except for its duration in time, consciousness lacks the properties of matter or energy even though it must be a product of both. We can neither weigh it nor transform it into anything further. It is the unique transparency of consciousness that enables us to perceive the existence and nature of the world. In this extraordinary attribute, consciousness is distinct from whatever ulterior reality we take it to report. The ontological status of consciousness has never been clarified to everyone's satisfaction, and perhaps it never will be.

Consciousness offers us a unique window on the world precisely because it is not like what it reveals. Observers could not continue to be what they are if their mental world had to *become* whatever they were *seeing*. In distinguishing a *datum* as essentially different from whatever that datum signifies, one places oneself squarely in the dualistic camp. This distinction is not universally accepted. The idea that consciousness and matter are different states of being leaves monistic thinkers uneasy. Materialists reduce consciousness to its physical basis, while idealists reduce the physical world to a conscious experience. A monist of either kind has trouble accounting for the differences that compel a dualist to distinguish consciousness from its physical basis in the brain and from the objects it discerns in the physical world.

Physics and neurophysiology support this distinction. Conscious vision is a response to photons reflected from an external object to retinal receptors. The resulting neural impulses are relayed to the visual cortex, where the act of seeing is consummated. But the contents of our visual field nevertheless do not *constitute* the external world; they only *picture* it. When we see the moon, our visual image is simply a *sign* of its existence in space a quarter of a million miles away. When we hear someone talking, the sound of the speaker's voice is something quite different from the air waves that impinge on our ears. As an insubstantial interface between subject and object, between the organism and its world, consciousness enables sky-watchers to experience an external physical world and even to picture an imaginary man in the moon.

Consciousness as such is simply a presence, but as a sign of something else, it has *meaning*, for it reveals the existence of the world. In order to make our way in that world, we need to interpret the data that consciousness offers us. Only when correctly interpreted do the luminous disks in the sky mean the sun and the moon. But interpretations can be wrong, and often are. If we want to stay "in touch with reality," as the phrase goes, we need to revise our interpretations by further investigation and checking with other observers. Some interpretations are irreconcilable. Except for the data (in any case provisional) that are reported by scientific method, a universal consensus is impossible in the face of our endless individual perspectives. Philosophy and religion supply more than enough examples. In itself, consciousness therefore offers nothing more than just what appears. But, as interpreted, its data can either inform or deceive us—or even do both at once.

Human consciousness has other limits. For instance, we cannot experience directly the inner world of another being. We observe the bodies and behavior of others, but never their perceptions or thoughts. We infer the inner life of others through their words and actions—and then not always correctly—by analogy with our own. We cannot, of course, directly experience the Freudian id, ego, and superego, for these are abstract concepts in his theoretical scheme of personality. And while it is generally accepted that awareness requires the activity of the brain, no one observing a living brain has ever detected the awareness that the brain is believed to produce. The neurochemical correlates of behavior are physical links in an elaborate chain not available to consciousness.

Self-consciousness is another peculiarly human development. We can direct attention not only to what we are aware of, but to the fact that we are aware, and finally toward ourselves as the persons we are, or believe that we are. To be self-conscious has therefore come to mean not only that we are aware of ourselves; it also implies a concern—often a disquieting concern—about our self-image and how we appear to others. Our bodies merely sense what is painful or pleasurable, but when self-esteem is at stake, we cannot be indifferent to how we are judged. Preoccupation with self-image limits our ability to see ourselves as a whole. Our psychological reactions relate to the entire organism, for it is only as unitary beings, not as organs or limbs, that we think or love or hate. Muscles and glands participate in that wholeness by giving physical expression to our feelings and enabling us to interact with the world.

In sickness or in health, we express ourselves through bodily metaphors. It clarifies the psychosomatic or mind-body problem to see that mind is not something separate from body but the sum of one's resources in action. When the psyche cannot achieve its aims directly, it develops *symptoms* in the form of reactions that may be physical, mental, or both. Frustrated motives, which are as physical and real as the organism that harbors them, can create tension, anger, exhaustion, or illness. Experiences of existential defeat promote depression or diminished function of the immune system, and everyone is more vulnerable to illness when self-esteem or hope is crushed. The physician who ignores the language of the body has not fully understood the patient. The heart not only pumps blood; it is the organ of passion that throbs with love, anger, or anxiety. The digestive system not only processes food; it registers preference, satisfaction, or rejection. Disgust causes vomiting; inability to release causes constipation; pent-up suffering or anger flow out in diarrhea. When an abrupt stress surpasses our endurance, we faint; and when contact with the world is too irritating, the skin becomes inflamed. Any organ or function can speak for the psyche when we cannot express ourselves in words. The psyche communicates not only by emitting and receiving sound waves, but by altering organ function. All organs react in some fashion to the directives of the psyche.

To conceive mind as the unifying organization of a living being is not a new idea. Aristotle defined the psyche as "the cause and first principle of the living body" (*On the Soul* 2.4). But not everyone sees the psyche as superordinate to the soma. The American Psychiatric Association's *Introductory Textbook of Psychiatry* (Andreassen and Black) describes the field as an attempt "to understand how aberrations in behavior are rooted in underlying biological mechanisms." Even Francis Crick, the Nobel laureate molecular biologist, has written:

> 'You', your joys and sorrows, your memories and your ambitions, your sense of personal identity and free will, are in fact no more than the behavior of a vast assembly of nerve cells and their associated molecules.
>
> *The Astonishing Hypothesis: The Search for the Soul*

Here are experts, impressed by the processes of nature, confidently giving mechanism primacy over the meaning that gives mechanism its significance. Mental life might not be possible without brain activity, but to think of the two as identical is to confuse the machinery of mind with the meaning conveyed by that machinery. Conscious living depends on physical processes in the brain but cannot be reduced to them.

The psyche acts as an integrated whole, but its unifying function is not a simple process. Its varied activities reach awareness selectively, some of them only at times and some of them not at all. Memories ordinarily lie dormant until they are needed, while for certain memories and processes, the barriers to awareness may be impassable. The human psyche nevertheless exhibits enough dynamic coherence and historical continuity to make us conscious centers of living experience.

For all the contribution that consciousness makes to our existence, it cannot grasp the complex dynamic that underlies and limits it. In consequence, we are impulsive, we overlook what we need to face, we disrespect our opponents, and we invite anxiety. In short, we fail to integrate our discordant motives. The complexity of the psyche is further evident in our dreams, which harbor motives, feelings, and conflicts that the conscious self can incorporate only with difficulty if at all. These half-buried or unacknowledged components form a "not-self" that contributes to the tensions and contradictions of all human behavior. Yet we cannot deny that, with all its limitations, our conscious dimension is what gives life its meaning and value. No matter how much we regret our transitory nature, if it were not for consciousness, we could never experience what makes existence the astonishing and sometimes misdirected adventure that it is.

ON MENTAL DISORDER

Man's inhumanity to man continues to the present day in the treatment of the mentally ill. Twenty percent of the population shows signs of psychiatric disorder, yet misconceptions and prejudices abound. The world knows little and cares less about these people, who are difficult to work with, politically powerless, and economically burdensome. Their fate is unlikely to improve in the foreseeable future, because even professionals are limited, not only in their ability to help patients, but in their power to influence authorities who are more concerned with their public image than with mental health. Diagnosis is often too hasty to be accurate. The system of care values cost above human need. Uninsured patients are denied treatment or shunted from one agency to another. Continuity of care is difficult to arrange. Patients who break the law are treated first as criminals and second as patients, if their illness is even acknowledged. Thousands remain confined or are left to shift for themselves.

The very concept of mental disorder, even if some find it controversial, denotes a reality that cannot be shrugged off as simply subjective opinion. Underestimating this reality shuts our eyes to an incalculable amount of suffering and wasted life, whether the symptoms are immediately obvious or not. However defined, mental disorder reveals a significant degree of discord between the psyche and the self-image. Lost in the grip of anxiety and the ambiguities of language, the troubled patient feels sinned against even while he sins against himself and others. At the same time, those who would like to help are hindered by the limits of their own personalities and the complexity of the task.

Endless problems result from failure to give young people the understanding and support they need during their developmental years. The outcome is often a major disorder of living such as mental illness or crime. In advanced cases, even the combined efforts of education, psychiatry, and the law have had scant influence. Institutional confinement and the correction of disordered brain chemistry achieve limited results but cannot prevent or relieve the underlying causes. Disorders as deeply rooted in relationship as in biology call for treatment guided by accurate understanding on the part of both the professions and the families.

The psychiatrist Thomas Szasz has tried to define mental illness out of existence by asserting that the term "illness" applies only to organic conditions. This is an arbitrary and unsound distinction. Szasz maintains that the concept of mental illness confuses symbolic behavior with organic disease and turns psychiatry into a political weapon for suppressing deviance. Certain self-appointed theorists have even considered schizophrenia a pseudo-illness created by social labeling. Such theorists are confusing their ideologies with science.

A subjective element nevertheless has to play a part in the diagnosis of mental disorder because, among other things, the diagnostician must decide to what extent a patient fails to consider his own welfare and the welfare of others. Judgments in this regard raise issues that are not only medical, but legal and moral. Society still draws a distinction between the "bad," who deserve punishment because they ought to know better, and the "sick," who deserve treatment because they presumably cannot help or understand what they are doing. (In California, the courts rule on patients' sanity and therefore their legal culpability solely on whether they can state in words the difference between right and wrong.) This problematic distinction creates more dilemmas for the law than for medicine, but it frequently baffles both professions.

Zealous libertarians can be so concerned with the patient's right to freedom that they forget his suffering. The inability of some patients to articulate their suffering makes it no less real. What does the patient gain by putting the right to remain sick ahead of the right to recover health? Well-informed realism is a better guide to care than ignorant benevolence. Intelligent treatment never neglects the patient's life as a whole. A serious mental disorder needs to be treated, even though the diagnosis may subject the patient to such unwelcome consequences as social stigma, confinement, and even the quarrels of dissenting experts.

The diagnostic system of the American Psychiatric Association aims to make diagnosis more scientific by eliminating subjective bias, yet many of its currently listed disorders are not well-defined objective entities but traditional clusters of symptoms adorned with new and impressive names. The system is necessarily provisional, always open to controversy, and periodically in need of revision. Diagnostic labeling has its limitations as well as its uses. By recognizing only proven organic causes and specifying diagnostic criteria with numerical precision, the system pursues an elusive objective validity while omitting the data needed for an adequate understanding of the patient's illness.

As mental disorder involves the whole person, so does sound diagnosis. Although certain mental disorders are clearly based on brain pathology, it is an error to assume that all mental disorder is evidence of brain disease. Organic pathology, formative experience, and the life predicament can all combine to generate symptoms. A diagnosis that overlooks any of these elements ignores the unity of the organism with its world, since brain activity affects experience, and experience affects brain activity. A psychiatric diagnosis rests on behavior characterized by three specific features: the behavior in question is adverse to the interests of the patient and the community; it is resistant to conscious control; and it demonstrates clear impairment of communication, foresight, and judgment.

Clinicians cannot afford to stop at a symptom diagnosis if they want to understand the patient as something more than a walking syndrome. When they prescribe medication before they understand the patient's formative experience and unsuccessful mode of living, they are treating symptoms instead of persons. Psychiatric disorder is too complex, socially and biologically, to be understood or treated by formula. The patient should always be understood and treated as a unique whole.

Separating the "mental" from the "physical" prejudices the care of all patients. The word *patient* (Latin for one who undergoes or suffers) implies no specific etiology, and the term is therefore misunderstood if used to restrict psychiatry to organic pathology. Even brain-damaged people have meaningful reactions and feelings that proper treatment must take into account. Experts may disagree on whether the psychological or biological dimension is more fundamental, but they at least recognize that both are essential for adequate diagnosis and treatment. It will ultimately cost us more than regret if the relevant psychosocial forces are overlooked on the simplistic assumption that nothing is involved but cerebral pathology.

In disregard of science and common sense, health insurance companies like to separate treatment of the biological and the psychosocial, because they prefer to pay for the treatment of physical conditions rather than the more costly mental disorders. Economic interests then become primary, while human need takes second place or is even disregarded. Another dubious practice has also increased, as the physician prescribes medication primarily for symptom control and delegates psychotherapy to a less expensive assistant. This practice diminishes the roles of both physician and therapist.

Since psychotherapy has not proved to be a cure-all, the equally limited effectiveness of psychotropic drugs has become the mainstay of present-day treatment. Correcting abnormal neurochemistry can sometimes alleviate certain symptoms, even though the results are often unpredictable. It will nevertheless be unfortunate if the current preoccupation of both professionals and the public with "chemical imbalance" blinds them to a patient's significant errors in living. One must never overlook the striving for health that underlies the symptoms. Reactions that at first seem purely pathological may serve needs that have not yet been recognized or met; such reactions need to be supported once their function is understood. If patients are to obtain the assistance they deserve, treatment cannot be limited to biochemistry. Their life experience and innate potentialities are of equal or greater importance. Medication and psychotherapy are at best complementary; neither can replace the other in dealing with refractory forms of mental disorder.

Treatment in a well-run hospital has a useful place. Stinting on hospital care turns indigent psychiatric patients into homeless drifters who spend much of their lives in and out of jail. These days, even patients who can afford hospitalization must accept hasty diagnosis and hasty discharge, with uncertain relief and frequent readmission. Whatever the defects of state mental hospitals in the past, patients could at least stay until they were ready to leave. When a well-trained staff is free to use its best judgment, hospitalization can provide therapeutic experience, and in the long run is cost-effective.

The problem of schizophrenia requires special attention. In this complex group of disorders, still far from adequately understood, biological susceptibility and difficulties in living are inseparable. Not surprisingly, organic brain defects have been demonstrated in patients with gross psychological limitations. In some cases, neurodevelopmental damage was probably present even before birth. Inconspicuous problems in communication or neurological function are sometimes observable in family members, who nevertheless need not display overt mental disorder. For potential schizophrenics, adolescence and young adulthood form a period of special risk. Biological predisposition probably makes it difficult for them to handle any degree of anxiety. Their self-esteem is predictably defective and unequal to the humiliations and defeats that most of us somehow endure.

Once overt symptoms appear, the patient has lost the ability to maintain a unified self. The field of consciousness can no longer be reserved exclusively for the self. Previously excluded from awareness, a subliminal mental world or "not-self" now openly divulges repressed motives that the constricted self could never acknowledge. These motives invade waking life in the form of delusions (unrealistic beliefs), hallucinations (internal sense perceptions taken for external realities), or unpredictable impulses that reduce the self to an impotent observer. Anxiety is reduced so far as the self can rationalize the psychotic intrusions, something at which paranoid patients are most skillful; but when the self finds the intrusions intolerable, anxiety may become overwhelming.

Defenses incompatible with an already fragile self-image jeopardize the patient's perception of reality. Such is the case when an episode of sexual humiliation makes a man feel so inadequate as a male that a latent passive-feminine attitude may emerge toward men whom he envies or fears, culminating in a so-called "homosexual panic" or a paranoid schizophrenic state. This pathological reaction is not to be confused with healthy homosexuality.

The deep-seated anxiety present in schizophrenics is sometimes overlooked. Typical of schizophrenia is the compulsion to placate a feared parental image by sacrificing the right to be oneself. The threat of this insistent urge, which the patient feels unable either to accept or resist, elicits rage and anxiety of a degree too intense for normal existence. At times it reaches an intolerable extreme, but often it is masked by psychotic defenses. It is nevertheless always present, and any increase in anxiety leads to an increase in psychotic behavior. (Psychosis is defined as a grossly defective grasp of reality.)

The patient's inevitable sense of personal failure destroys any hope of healthy intimacy or communication, while despair makes suicide an ever-present option. Delusional preoccupations—commonly in the fields of sex, aggression, or religion—compensate many patients for their inability to achieve any realistic fulfillment. Such psychotic defenses enable many a schizophrenic to keep on living, but only at the expense of renouncing the life they otherwise could have had.

Psychotic behavior varies from patient to patient. No one can work in a mental hospital without discovering that the schizophrenic label is applied to patients whose differences outweigh their similarities. Psychotic communication makes collaborating with the most disturbed patients all but impossible for many well-meaning helpers, especially for untrained beginners. Yet even grossly delusional patients are willing to talk once they sense that the listener is trustworthy, a person who tries to understand without jumping to conclusions. Such was a patient with whom I worked for several years; his story follows.

At a university outpatient clinic, I was assigned a schizophrenic patient whose brother had brought him straight from a month in the workhouse. Divorce had left Quentin* deeply humiliated and doubting his already impaired sense of manliness. In his search for help, he met a spiritualist who introduced him to automatic writing (writing without conscious plan or control), an activity he performed with surprising ease. On one fateful occasion he tried to stop the writing but found he could no longer control it. He threw the pencil across the room but felt the words flow down his arm and take charge of his behavior. Although inaudible, the power of these words compelled him to give up any gainful employment. Unable to make support payments, he was hauled into court, where the judge dismissed his unlikely story and sentenced him to 30 days in the workhouse.

Quentin sensed that he was mentally ill, but this insight was not curative. When he said anything "they" disapproved of, he flinched as though struck in the face. Electroconvulsive treatments were ineffective, and I stopped them at his request. He told me later that it was only after I did so that he began to trust me. He frequently felt an invisible body riding on his shoulders. At times he felt the presence of others so vividly that, although living alone, he set the table for them. "They" exercised ruthless control over his behavior and kept telling him, "You shall obey." When he once started to go to a movie despite their disapproval, they twisted his head so forcibly that he had to turn back lest they break his neck.

He wrote the following description of his psychotic experience with graphic clarity and an exceptional degree of insight:

---

*The name of this patient and all others are of course fictitious.

I cannot say because I do not know if or not it was one thing or a chain of events that began in childhood which caused my eventual mental illness but whichever it may have been the fact remains I surely lost controle [*sic*] of my own mind. Because I did lose controle [*sic*] of my mind it acts, thinks, and operates separately and independently of me and my will. One of the worst things about it is that it acts in ways that are not practical in any economical sense but in ways that are in reverse to any sensible, logical, reasonable adult manner. Assuming then that all the experiences, teachings and environments of childhood have a direct influence upon it, it would seem reasonable to think that its actions are only childish attempts to solve serious adult problems and childish ways of escaping those problems. Therefore it seems to me that something other than shock therapy or just analysis is definately [*sic*] in order.

Quentin improved, left the hospital, and continued to see me, but it took years before he could report certain relevant childhood information. After seven years of therapy, he came in for his usual outpatient session to explain that he could not fully occupy the chair because he felt a child sitting beside him and a grown person behind him holding him down. As we talked, he embarked on a recital of memories he had never shared before. The central theme was his lack of self-assurance and his cowardice in the presence of other men, attitudes evidently based on his upbringing. When he was nine, he and his brother were caught masturbating. "I never felt so ashamed in all my life. . . . I burned for a week or more. They preached in my head that it would drive me crazy. . . . I worried about it for fifteen years or more." He had never before told this to anyone and drew a deep breath to say he now felt better. All his life he had felt, "I'm lacking in something. I just don't come up even with them [other men]. I can't meet them on equal terms. . . . I feel condemned, sentenced. . . . You're down. You stay down. It's like stepping on a cockroach, filthy son-of-a-bitch thing. Kill him. . . . I can actually see [meaning 'picture'] a cockroach running on the floor, going in every direction, and some big monstrous human going to step on it." As our interview ended, he suddenly exclaimed with surprise, "The child isn't there now!" Child and adult had reunited at last.

We finally learned that the all-powerful "they" perpetuated the words and attitudes of the adults who had terrified Quentin throughout his childhood. His symptoms served, as he had already surmised, to allay the anxiety created by consciously trying to be an adult while unconsciously condemned to retreat to the role of a submissive child.

The patient in the next example is a borderline psychotic but not schizophrenic. The pervasive nature of Ariel's illness makes her far more resistant to therapy than Quentin was. Consumed by hate and self-hate from her early years, she can form no fulfilling intimacy with others and, despite achieving limited rapport with a therapist, is unable to surrender her pathology.

Ariel lives in a state of constant anxiety. She sees herself as a "freak" because of her supposedly abnormal appearance (symbolic of her self-estimate) that she cannot believe is unnoticed by others. She cannot endure being who she is and wants desperately to be someone she is not—an obviously impossible wish. She never leaves the house without a time-consuming effort to present a perfect appearance, but she often gives up trying in sheer disgust. She also suffers from a phobic reaction to "dirt," visible or invisible, and her idiosyncratic cleaning compulsion makes for constant friction with her family.

Ariel warned her therapist from the start that she would never change. As she put it, "It's this way or no way," if she is to survive at all. Although touched by the suffering of others, especially nonhuman creatures (she hates the human race), she derives no satisfaction from her own talents or virtues. Except for brief and unpredictable moments, she cannot count on carrying out any plan, since every impulse is countered by its opposite. She once had an out-of-body experience and has always regretted that her spirit did not leave her body for good, because she "never really belonged in this world." Filled with a constant "sense of foreboding, hopelessness and fear," she alternates between rage and anxious despair. She demonstrates her characteristic combination of self-will and self-hate in her repeated and deliberate rejections of help. Her feeling of ugliness allows her no hope and no future. "The hurt in my life is in my very core, you might say even in my soul. I can't escape it. I can't fight it. It is *there,* never to leave me." She believes that whoever denies her ugliness is just trying to spare her, but when anything reminds her of it, she is devastated. It is her belief that disgust or horror are the only reactions others could have toward her appearance. Unshakably convinced that her ugliness is "the truth," she cannot separate her body image from her diminished estimate of what she is worth. As she puts it, "I want a new life, but there are no miracles and I'm not going to get it."

At an early age she felt rejected by others and began to reject herself. She feels her trouble had to come from "fate" or from committing some nameless crime in a previous incarnation. She defends her way of living as necessary to prevent the "shock" of being shamed by unexpected rejection. She once suffered panic when a child's casual remark made her feel intolerably ugly. Never having received the warmth and acceptance for which she longed in vain, she stored her anger in one compartment and her sense of worthlessness in another. While needing the love of people whom she still resents, at an early age she adopted their negative attitude as her own, thereafter using her preoccupation with ugliness to punish both them and herself. Shame protects her from the risk of hoping, yet her shame is contradicted by a secret hope that she cannot entirely renounce. Although she claims she only wants to look "normal," her psyche harbors a compensatory vanity, an unconscious longing for perfection, that makes her hate her actual appearance even though it is in fact quite acceptable.

Ariel was temporarily assigned an inexperienced therapist who refused a small gift she offered when she learned he was leaving the area. From her perspective, accepting her gift meant accepting *her,* and rejecting her gift meant rejecting *her.* She therefore not only took his refusal to mean she was "no good"—a judgment of her own that she could not tolerate when it came from others—but at the same time interpreted his refusal as *proof* that she was no good. Even after she realized that he had misunderstood her motives, she turned his misunderstanding against herself. In situations of this kind she has an urge to cut herself, because bleeding is the only way she can convey to others how deeply she suffers.

Yet she resists taking the simplest steps to get better. If anything helps her, she stops it. Her rationalization: "What's the use?" She survives by substituting self-will for self-respect. Consciously feeling unable to change, she asserts her autonomy by a stubborn refusal to work toward health. What could have been a healthy impulse of self-assertion is diverted instead to self-punishment. This unconscious tactic spares her the tension that would undoubtedly accompany an effort to get well. Yet she cannot—will not—see that her way of life is not a destiny but a choice. Anxiety results from evading responsibility for the decision to express both her anger and her guilt through self-hatred. The obsession with being a "freak" conveys the pathetic bizarreness of her defensive response to her childhood suffering.

A therapist who opposes her self-will threatens her right to be herself and her need for "protection." One who is reluctant to resist her destructive self-will permits her to stay sick. Nothing but the most determined resolve on the part of both therapist and patient is likely to break the vicious circle of Ariel's existence. Ideal treatment would require not only strenuous encounters with a rigid and uncomprehending family, but an environment with both the formal authority and therapeutic skill to override her fear of giving up her self-destructive system of living. The current legal restrictions on hospitalization rule out involuntary placement of any length.

A third patient was correctly diagnosed as schizophrenic. Penny, a girl of eighteen, was admitted in a state of acute catatonic excitement. Since the episode was of limited duration, it would now be called schizophreniform. Fortunately I took shorthand notes as I interviewed her over a period of several days. Penny's psychotic communications made her prepsychotic lack of fulfillment unmistakable. They revealed the intensity of her unmet longings and her compensatory disregard of reality, a disregard interrupted by her "me" for a fleeting moment, as recorded in my notes. In the course of a summer she made a social recovery and returned to her prepsychotic state of propriety, shyness, and inhibition. The following are verbatim excerpts from her conversation. My words are in brackets.

I'm through with men. . . . I don't want any goddamn man. . . . They are all alike. . . . I don't know what you are writing down there and I don't care. . . . I've been drug through enough hell . . . I'm through with men . . . I told you you're playing with dynamite. . . . Where's my sundaes? Where's everything? [*Orders a dinner in great detail; her interest in eating and fulfillment has a positive prognostic import.*]
You've got the wrong person.
[You are the person we are interested in.]
You don't understand. I'm Melissa [*not her name*].
[Where is Penny? (*her name*)]
I'm helping her. I'm not doing anything. . . . You might say I understand men better . . . never could get along well with women.
[Why not?]
Maybe they were jealous of me, because I've been so many mistresses of so many men, Hitler, Mussolini, men of every continent, ever since time began.
[Are there any young men that interest you?]
I've got three of them picked out—no, more than three—I don't know. Albert E. I marry him. I choose him out of everybody else. . . . [*to the physician*] Make me five foot four inches or I'll divorce you. Himself to me we got married all over again this morning, but I didn't get the ring back. . . . Damn fool. One hundred ten . . . for I won't be satisfied till you leave me there.
[Where?]
Five foot four, dope! [*Pulls her hair, screeches at the top of her voice, goes on to prescribe desirable heights and weights for men and women, and demands a long list of luxury items.*]
[*Next day*] Hurry up. I want some action. By God, I can't wait. By God, that's an idea. Bite a piece out of them. It cured Gail. By God, I will. Joan. Bring her on. By God, YAHOOO! Then that goddamn June. By God, I can't YAHOO! By God, I can't wait to sink my teeth into them. [*These are girls she envies.*] Give them a good

swift kick—every one of them. By God, grandma, Hitler, some of them damn Frenchmen, some of them I had affairs with. I don't believe I'll bite the men. I'll just kick them. Yahoo! I might sock them. Yeez. Definitely! Yahoo! By God, wonderful! Yahoo!

[Untrained attendant: What if they have your teeth pulled?]

I shall sock you twice and kick you once. I know it does sound a little fiendish. . . . Oh, my God, my God, isn't this awful? [*momentary emergence of the prepsychotic self*] On second thought, I'll only hit you once. . . . You're up to no good. By God, you try anything with me and you're going to get shit. You remember that, both of you. . . . I mean it anyway. Damn you! AAOOO! OOOH! By God, you boys come down here, you're going to get shit . . . you too. Damn fool. I don't give a damn who you are . . . you can go straight to hell, both of you.

[Attendant: You have paint on your toenails, don't you?]

You're both goddamn shitty rats, both of you! . . . Why don't you go to one of my other twins? . . . If you don't, I'll tell Hitler. I'll tell Cyclops. No. Cyclops, you're Adolph. By God, I can't wait to hit you.

[*Four days later*] My God, what am I supposed to do, pretend to marry you or something?

[No.]

Oh, anything you say. My God, man. [*spitting at frequent intervals*] God, papa . . . My God . . . I don't know how long you have been having this pretense on, FDR [*Franklin Delano Roosevelt was then president*] and doctor and whoever you are. [*Note the simultaneous perception, here and later, of the physician as himself, as president, as father, and as husband.*] My God, I'm going to faint. You're supposed to have died and you don't die at all. My God, man, and to pull your daughter Penny out of something, you drug me into shitty hell and made me Aida. [*Aida symbolizes her fate of being existentially buried alive.*]

[Please explain what is going on.]

Well, you see, it's rather hard to explain. You see, Jack, Billie's brother, met me. . . . In reality, I'm Carole Lombard [*a well-known actress of the day*]. You see. Jack met me over in Japan and married me. And everybody else . . . You? Everybody is married to me. And tell me about Penny, because I'm the only one who can help her out of it. And you drug me down and gave me electricals and every other goddamn thing.

[*Next day*] I feel you understand why I'm being kept here. . . . You threw me into this goddamn sanitarium. . . . I know what's going on all the time.

[How does it seem?]

Very odd. Yes, very odd.

[Just how?]

You want my impression? I'll do better than that. I'll even write it out for you. [*writes but covers it with her left hand*] You have evidently used me to resurrect all these people. . . . I don't know whether to trust anyone or not . . . Yes, there's something I want to know while you're at it. I'm evidently this person called A-I-D-A.

[Could this all be a dream?]

It's definitely not part of a dream, you damn fool, you. Well, it isn't a dream. You're evidently making a movie. You're evidently letting me take the character Scarlett O'Hara in the sequel to 'Gone with the Wind.' You are evidently letting me play the part of Amber in 'Forever Amber.' A-I-D-A I believe was written by V-E-R-D-I. . . . It isn't make-believe. Cyclops . . . he was a Negro . . . my father . . .

[Your father was a Negro?]

Yes. You are my father . . . in Ethiopia. Both of you are my husbands. No, you're my father. . . . It's all mixed up.

[Naively trying to encourage insight, I ask: Like a dream?]

IT'S NOT A DREAM, GODDAMN YOU!

Well-meaning but inexperienced as I was at that point in my career, I should have waited to explore the patient's capacity for insight until she was in a stable convalescent phase and able to consider psychotherapy appropriate to her condition. Attempting conventional psychotherapy would have been an error, for it could offer nothing helpful for someone so immersed in her compensatory psychosis. What she needed was supportive understanding. My premature effort to promote insight misjudged her profound need to live her compensatory psychotic experience to the full. None of this could have been expressed or discharged through her constricted prepsychotic self. The electric convulsive treatment ordinarily applied in those days may have suppressed acute psychotic symptoms, but it did nothing to increase the patient's ability to handle life.

Formal psychotherapy is designed for patients who are both emotionally and intellectually ready for an experience that at best is difficult, and at times unavoidably painful. The following chapter on psychotherapy is addressed to nonpsychotic patients who are looking for help with an anxiety problem. This approach is advisable for someone ready for psychotherapy and willing to give it a serious try.

THE MEANING
OF ANXIETY

Oh would some power the giftie gie us
To see ourselves as others see us!
It would from many a blunder free us
And foolish notion.

Robert Burns, *To a Louse* (adapted)

With a poet's intuition, Burns understood the risks of failing to see ourselves as we really are. That error is conspicuous in the defensive but unacknowledged contradictions that create anxiety. Despite the frequency of this disorder, few people appreciate what it means or why it afflicts us when it does. Anxiety is a complication of living that its victims bring on themselves unwittingly; they are therefore unlikely to understand it without help. Since anxiety can mystify the ordinary observer, a full clarification is called for. The analysis that follows can be summarized in a sentence: anxiety arises when an instinctive effort to relieve insecurity serves instead to increase it.

In everyday language, anxiety refers to concerns of almost any kind, but in the present context we need a more specific definition. Anxiety is understood here as a disquieting apprehension for which

47

the sufferer cannot correctly account, because the feeling of anxiety blocks self-comprehension. The anxiety experience, in other words, never automatically brings understanding with it. Superficial observers have therefore concluded that anxiety has no psychological significance and can be dealt with solely as a disorder of the brain without personal meaning.

The biological component, which is undeniably important, dominates current theory and treatment. Neurons in the brain stem create the acute tension of panic states, and there is a significant degree of familial occurrence. The appeal of a biological explanation is reinforced by the fact that certain medications provide symptom relief, although the relief is seldom complete or curative. Although the biological findings are relevant, they do not explain why anxiety occurs when it does, or what those who feel it may be doing to bring it about. Biology is not the whole story.

Anxiety is symptomatic of a personality divided between permissible and impermissible aims. The problem begins early in life when certain motives are excluded from conscious awareness by excessive disapproval. Such disunity tends to be maintained indefinitely thereafter by a false self-image designed to ensure social approval and a measure of self-esteem. Anxiety occurs when there is any risk that the forbidden motives will regain their conscious role and invalidate the unrealistic self-image. (Note that Freud apparently overlooked the role of social disapproval as an essential precursor of human anxiety.)

Anxiety is not to be confused with guilt. Guilt feelings mark a conscious realization that one has done something forbidden. Anxiety comes into play only when one is unable to face the guilt feelings consciously.

Defensive behavior is an attempt to decrease overt anxiety by protecting one's self-image. The defense is not based on an accurate picture of a situation but on a feeling that one is under threat. Its inappropriateness is not recognized by the anxious person, for whom the defense is an instinctive act of self-protection. The defensive behavior ultimately complicates life by increasing the anxiety it is supposed to relieve.

In acute anxiety, people often experience some physical signs.

They will generally notice an increased heart rate, often accompanied by increased sweating. Such physiological reactions are sometimes overshadowed by defensive outbursts of irritation or anger. Changes are noticeable in posture, in facial expression, or in voice quality. Speech may be confused, excessive in some cases, inhibited in others. In severe cases, tension may become so intolerable that people feel they are "falling apart." Their hearts pound, they tremble, they cannot catch their breath, and they expect to die, go insane, or lose control.

Changes in behavior are nevertheless not always observed. Habitual character defenses can mask anxiety so well that the familiar signs are inconspicuous or absent. Common defense reactions of this order are chronic dependency, a habitual tendency to disparage, preoccupation with physical symptoms, or obsessional needs for perfection and control. The defensive function of such behavior is confirmed by its power to suppress overt anxiety, but so long as the underlying anxiety is unresolved, these defenses serve mainly to handicap or warp the personality.

Some experts hold that a "normal" level of anxiety improves performance, but anxiety as understood here never enhances one's efficiency. On the contrary, anxiety of any degree undermines both inner peace and objective performance, making it harder to think, speak or act as one would like. Conscious anxiety may range in severity from a faint disquiet at the margin of awareness to an overwhelming sense of panic.

Freud assumed that people instinctively fear their own primitive drives, which he called the id. The power of those drives is undeniable, but they create no anxiety when they are enacted with concern for oneself and others. The conflicts between innate drive and social adaptation are therefore acquired, not intrinsic. Since the biological drives are a necessary part of human nature, danger to self-esteem lies not in the drives themselves but in their misapplication. Anxiety is not inherent in the nature of a drive; it occurs when the drive is put to fraudulent or duplicitous use.

Irvin D. Yalom, an experienced psychotherapist, proposed that anxiety is a response to four existential predicaments that no human being can evade: the inevitability of death, the ultimate isolation of the individual, the difficulty of finding meaning in life, and the inescapable burden of freedom. It is nevertheless open to question whether these predicaments, formidable as they are, can be the true sources of pathological anxiety. There is evidence that the more we live a life guided by accurate self-knowledge rather than self-deception or pretense, the less we are apt to suffer from anxiety in the sense used here. This position will be amplified as we continue.

While anxiety indicates that self-esteem is threatened by a source that one cannot identify without appropriate help, feelings such as embarrassment reflect conduct that is readily recalled and consciously regretted. In this case, we either recognize our error at once or soon learn of it from others, to our subsequent benefit. Conscious anxiety, in contrast, is a more troubling problem, because we understand neither what it means nor what to do about it. Anxiety nevertheless shares with all humiliation a mistaken effort to evade some aspect of inner or outer reality. In his analysis of humility, the psychiatrist Hubert Benoît writes:

> My egotistical pretension towards the "on high" has to express itself in an unceasing process of imagination because it is false, and in *radical contradiction* with the reality of things. The whole problem of human distress is resumed in the problem of humiliation. . . . To cure distress is to be freed from all possibility of humiliation. Whence comes my humiliation? From seeing myself powerless? No, that is not enough. It comes from the fact that I try in vain not to see my real powerlessness. *It is not powerlessness itself that causes humiliation, but the shock experienced by my pretension to omnipotence when it comes up against the reality of things.* . . . The veritable cause of my distress is never in the outside world, it is only in the claim that I throw out and which is broken against the wall of reality. I deceive myself when I complain that the wall has hurled itself against me and has wounded me; it is I that have injured myself against it, my own action which has caused my suffering. When I no longer pretend, nothing will ever injure me again.
>
> *The Supreme Doctrine: Psychological Studies in Zen Thought*
> (italics in original)

The injury Benoit speaks of is of course emotional, the injury to pride. Some people assuage injured pride by proclaiming their superior status instead of doing what the situation demands. Legitimate pride is something else. Based on demonstrated competence, it is a sign of security and needs no bolstering by pretense. But people are subject to anxiety in proportion to the gap between what they are and what they think they are. That gap is apparent in discrepancies not only between what people tell others and what they tell themselves, but also in what they cannot admit to themselves even when it may be obvious to an observer.

Why don't we accept ourselves as we are? Human beings are born immature and take years to reach their full development. Most animals learn to look after themselves at an early age, whereas the human child requires care and supervision for many years, with consequences that tend to be permanent. Although this process has its advantages, it exacts a price. Even though a child soon learns to respond to the wishes of his caretakers, for a considerable period he lacks the discrimination that comes with growing intelligence and experience. On certain occasions the child resists or resents even appropriate control. Anxiety does not, however, result from insistence on discipline or clear behavioral guidelines. When parents exercise their authority in a spirit of empathy and love, their child grows up secure. But if they set impossible demands and are blind to the child's basic needs, they promote a very different outcome. When the child is forced to submit beyond his tolerance or understanding, his underlying motives are not abolished but repressed, and the frustrated child embarks on a life of unwitting duplicity.

People whose security depends on a fraudulent self-image are headed for trouble when the self cannot rise to the demands of the life situation. The rest of the psyche remains free of self-deception, because its accurate retention of everything it has ever experienced compels it to live by the truth, whatever the cost involved. The self, in contrast, cares less about honesty than about presenting an idealized image to the world.

Certain people think that by openly confessing their lack of self-esteem they excuse all their failings, but verbal confession in itself does nothing to correct errors in living. *We achieve true self-esteem only when we consistently treat others and ourselves with genuine respect.* Since people can respect others only insofar as they respect themselves, those who fail to live up to this requirement find it easier to substitute words for action. (Harry Stack Sullivan is worth reading on the issues of self-esteem and self-respect.) True respect means recognizing the intrinsic value of every person and ultimately of all that exists. We have every right to maintain our own interests and values so long as we recognize our true place in the order of things. Self-acceptance and self-transcendence are then integrated in a realistic self-appraisal that neither exaggerates nor minimizes what we actually are.

Although the chief purpose of the self is to maintain a positive self-image, it is further burdened with additional goals, such as physical survival and personal fulfillment. The difficulties of the self arise from this complex assignment, which may entrap it in a network of conflicting aims it can neither reconcile nor reject. Symptoms of mental disorder appear when the self is no longer able to harmonize these competing goals. When appropriate intentions drive one part of the personality, and inappropriate intentions drive another, the consequent loss of integrity is what lies at the heart of anxiety.

While everyone is capable of feeling anxiety, people vary in susceptibility because of their differences in genetic makeup and life experience. People predisposed to anxiety have a characteristic approach to life. Sensitive, perfectionistic yet willful, such types expect the worst, partly because of genetic makeup and partly because of social conditioning. Their dread of disapproval is fed by low self-esteem and reinforced by their ambivalent dependence on those whose approval they desire. At a deeper level, they resent those whom they feel compelled to please. Believing their self-effacement entitles them to special consideration, they harbor unreasonable expectations that add to their insecurity. Their conscious need for reassurance masks a covert self-will so strong that that it humiliates them to submit to the demands of normal living.

Such pathology is likely to develop in children who find that being true to themselves subjects them to intolerable disapproval or rejection. At that point they face a critical dilemma: to earn acceptance they must be false to themselves; by being true to themselves they forfeit the acceptance they need from others. Failure to resolve this dilemma precludes true self-esteem. To put the child's dilemma into words:

> *I need you to love me just as I am. If you don't, I must choose between living for your sake and living for my sake, but being forced to make this choice paralyzes my freedom to be what I need to be.*

This dilemma is based on the need to master two roles that are equally indispensable in a social world. One role (here called the "you") requires identifying oneself with others; the other role (here called the "me") requires being true to oneself. The psyche needs to reconcile the "you" with the "me," even though they may be in conflict, because both roles are essential to being fully human. Identifying with others is necessary for a social existence, and positive self-regard is necessary if life is to be worth living at all. Mental health requires achieving a successful balance of these two fundamental aims. Failure in this effort is a predictable pathway to anxiety.

When a child has no way to extricate herself from a dilemma of this kind, she may finally arrive at the following position:

> *How can I love myself when those whose love I need find me unworthy? I hate them for not loving me, and I hate myself for being unworthy. I wish I could love them, but I can't. Because I am unable to love, I can neither deserve love nor accept it. If only I could live without love altogether—but I can't.*

The stage may even be set for psychosis or suicide when the desperate child concludes:

> *To be what you want me to be will destroy me, but to be what I want to be will destroy you. I cannot live with you and I cannot live without you.*

It may be useful to present some clinical examples to make the experience and meaning of anxiety more vivid and intelligible.

Beatrice was an intelligent and gifted young woman whose life was scarred by severe anxiety. She oscillated for years between anxiety, depression, and rebellious anger. Her adult experience forcefully revives the helpless confusion of an insecure child and shows how essential—and how difficult—it is for such a child to gain the right to be herself. She was a first child, born at a time when her mother was secretly unhappy about difficulties in her marriage. In their inexperience and self-absorption, both parents failed to recognize and respond to Beatrice's feelings, which she largely concealed except for occasional outbursts of anger. She grew up ambitious but insecure and impulsive. When the last and best of three marriages finally failed, she fell into despair. Her impassioned report, which follows, throws a detailed and instructive light on the struggle to get well.

When from earliest life you grow up as if you don't matter, the hurt and bottomless perplexity settle down through the tiniest cracks of your being, a permeating cloud which is indistinguishable from "you," since you don't know who you are. You are nothing. . . . Hungry and hollow and hurt. A big aching nothing. I wasn't abused or beaten or locked in the basement as a child. I was nothing. But something was after me. For as long as I can remember I've been driven and pushed. I talked too fast, ate too fast, did everything too fast. . . .

Now, decades later, . . . something horrible was happening to me, but I was the one, in my eternal impulsiveness, who had made it happen. I initiated a divorce, then panicked and wanted to undo it. My husband's unwillingness to give me "another chance" (understandably, since I had put him through this once before) threw me into the worst panic of my life. His "rejection" was a divine punishment, a sign of my absolute damnation. I had hurt him, failed him, driven him away because of my craziness. I was repulsive, untouchable, a leper. Repellent, a horrible person, a monster. A mess, hopeless, sick, unsalvageable. *Therefore I was getting what I deserved.* To suffer unjustly is one thing, but to suffer because you deserve to is unbearable. My punishment was to be unloved—forever. This was the fate worse than death I'd been running from all my life, and now it was here. I deserved it. "You're selfish the way some people are born without an appendix," my husband told me. I was horrified because he was right. . . . I felt I had no choice but to die. Instead of trying to kill myself outright, though, I wanted to run to the emergency room and demand that they put me out, make me unconscious. I couldn't stand being awake inside my own head. My repulsiveness gave me chills and my despair filled me with terror. I couldn't endure it one more second. I had been killed but couldn't lose consciousness. My curse was to be dead and alive. . . .

The guilty sinful shameful creature who had caused so much hurt and suffered so much hurt could not stop crying. She was out in the open and wouldn't go back. She had emerged mute and stupefied, like Kasper Hauser, the young man who mysteriously showed up in the town of Nuremberg in 1828 after growing up confined to a cellar; he had never learned to use language. He knew nothing. I knew too much, but none of it helped. I had been trying to do things "right" my whole life (Little Miss Straight A's) but whatever I did was never right or never enough.

Little Miss Straight A's had always been articulate and analytical, but she had wrecked her life all the same. Her knowledge was useless so long as Kasper Hauser stayed locked in the basement. Until now I had been one or the other, at one moment abounding with insight that made my despair unreal, at another moment crushed by despair that made my insight unreal. When Kasper Hauser came out and stayed out, Little Miss Straight A's was aghast. There was no other way for all of me to hear and to learn, so long as Kasper Hauser stayed locked in the cellar. . . .

Once I made a trembling overture to my husband by sending a brief note and felt that my gesture was just right. In a rare state of feeling at peace, I decided to go for a walk. Five minutes into the walk, the sky fell on my head. In a creepy burst of horror, I realized that one word in my message was "wrong." The discovery came while I was obsessively re-playing every word of the message in my head, trying to reassure myself that it was "right."

The realization that I had used the wrong word . . . terrified me . . . I was frantic. I had used the wrong word, confirmed that I was truly selfish. Now my husband must despise me more than ever, and my life was ruined. My parents tried to reassure me that my life wasn't ruined because of one wrong word, but I knew I was beyond hope, unredeemable. In the midst of a call, my father said something that stunned me: *You think you aren't good enough, so you try too hard.*

These words came like air entering a sealed catacomb or the lifting of an ancient curse. It was . . . a miracle . . . to *know what I was doing.* It isn't that I hadn't "known," but it was only Little Miss Straight A's who knew. My gibbering idiot, my Kasper Hauser, had known nothing but dumb grief. . . .

Then another thought popped into my head: maybe I had said the wrong thing deliberately. . . . I had to find out if I could afford to be human and still deserve to be loved. . . . I was actually trying out how it would feel to give myself the right to make a mistake.

I was swimming in the mixed waters of self-blame and self-forgiveness, crying in a flood, but for the first time the momentum was more relief than terror. . . . The more I allowed myself to feel that *I deserved to live no matter what horrible things I had done*, the more I cried. These tears were different from any others. My entire being was coming into the open with the tears as they poured through the gates.

Then [in a phone conversation with my father] a sensation came over me that seemed unconnected to what we were talking about. I dreaded having to hang up the phone when the conversation would be over. I knew we would eventually have to hang up. My dread increased every moment. I was sitting on the floor looking at the long phone cord, desolate, crying ever more uncontrollably. I wouldn't be able to stand it when we hung up. I would die when we hung up. There would be nothing left.

At that moment I broke through, completely involuntarily, to being a child. . . . I felt physically as if I were five or six years old. The exact quality of the grief shocked me because I recognized it instantly even though it was from so long ago. The relief was unspeakable. Something infinitely precious was being restored to me. I kept saying, "I'm heartbroken, I'm heartbroken." All I could do was say the words over and over. . . .

My child-self came into consciousness, effortlessly and unexpectedly, several more times in the days that followed, most intensely when I relived a temper tantrum. I began to shake and rock back and forth and without making a sound . . . I let loose a bottomless fount of rage. My adult self was present in the child's agony, observing and sympathizing . . . and understanding and rejoicing. The deliverance of finding myself, meeting myself, can only be called joy.

Now I knew where I got the creepy sinister lifelong feeling of being cursed, a monster. I reached for paper and pencil, taking dictation from my soul, and wrote in shaking capital letters: GRIEF REPULSIVE ANGER OBNOXIOUS. These words were me. They were my childhood. I was able to write them because I was seeing myself at the same time from inside and outside. I finally understood, not just in my head but through and through, I am enraged because my misery makes me repulsive to others.

I have reached within and discovered that I'm not a monster. I have met and accepted the creature who felt like a monster and now I know, because I've seen for myself, that it isn't a monster, it's a child torn with suffering. . . .

I no longer feel I'm supposed to be purging myself of grief, anger and terror as if I were exorcising demons. Over the years I would have a panic attack, survive it, feel relief . . . and bounce back to self-confidence. . . . Sooner or later I would always plunge back into the nightmare—because I was always trying to get rid of the bad stuff. I have learned that it's exactly the opposite: I needed to embrace the monster and welcome her into the fold.

This woman's story fits the so-called "borderline" disorder, a diagnosis applied more often to women, in whom the self is destabilized by its contradictory subsystems. The pattern begins in sensitive children who, lacking an assured conviction of their inner worth, reach adolescence eager to place responsibility for their happiness on an idealized partner whose "love" will supply what is missing. Their subsequent course is marked by rashly undertaken sexual or marital adventures destined for regret. Periods of precarious security last only until unrealistic expectations and human failings in both partners collide in mutual disillusion. As the illusions fall away, the patient feels abandoned, humiliated, betrayed, enraged, and desperate—emotions born of her presentiment that she can count on no reliable support, either within herself or from others. Each new crisis revives the helplessness of childhood, sometimes in the form of physical distress.

A patient like Beatrice justifies her desperate response by assuming that she has the right and should have the power to relieve her suffering. In that effort, she feels driven toward three different goals at once: to regain the love of the person she lost, to retaliate for being abandoned, and to atone for her impulsive errors. She thereafter vacillates between self-condemnation (because the rejection is deserved) and self-righteous anger (for not receiving the love to which she feels entitled). The need to escape this emotional see-saw culminates in contradictory and unrealistic demands for omnipotent control.

Such a patient will face a long and anguished struggle to accept responsibility for her mode of living. To break the vicious cycle, she must re-experience her early suffering without shame or self-hate, and stop entrusting her self-esteem to those whom she has assigned the roles of saviors or surrogate parents. She will achieve genuine health only by discovering that her value rests on accepting what she is, not on trying to exercise unrealistic control over herself or others.

An anxiety-driven existence makes life a nightmare from which one awakens only by dealing with the futile modes of defense at its root. Yet few things can be more difficult than deciding whether to retain or renounce a lifelong defense. Perfectionists suffer tormenting indecision when they discover that their system of preserving pride in fact endangers pride, and that a facade of invulnerability keeps them vulnerable.

Once understood, however, *conscious* anxiety can be useful, for it teaches people what they need but have not yet learned to face. An unexplained pounding of the heart, for example, should prompt one to look inward. It means that one is making, or on the verge of making, an unwise move whose motives are being ignored and whose consequences will be regretted.

Consider an intelligent man who planned to marry an attractive divorcee with small children. As the wedding day came near, he felt anxiety for which he could find no reason. When he nevertheless went ahead with the marriage, the reason for his anxiety quickly appeared. To his great chagrin, he discovered how jealous he felt of his new wife's children. To save the marriage, he had to swallow his pride and confront a narcissistic element in his makeup that he had never suspected.

Anxiety can therefore be an invaluable warning, but only if one deciphers the message correctly. Treating it as a purely physical event overlooks its interpersonal purpose as an evasion of reality, a defensive maneuver that patients cannot easily acknowledge and renounce.

Since people do not know the true sources of their anxiety, they turn with some relief to a preoccupation with symbolic fears. These often take the form of concern about one's health or even a fear of dying. It is easy to settle on fears of physical illness, because a physical disorder becomes the responsibility of a physician, and one is thereby relieved of confronting what one is not eager to face. Physical illness also has social respectability, a status that psychiatric disorder has not yet acquired. The fear of dying carries a still deeper meaning. In the young, it means a fear of life. In the old, it means having to recall one's irremediable regrets with little time left for making amends.

Clarice is a young mother completely overwhelmed by unrealistic fears about her physical health. Convinced that her brain is damaged and her chemistry is abnormal, she still comes for an initial psychiatric consultation even though she believes that treatment for anxiety is a waste of time because her illness is purely physical. She feels that she is beyond help, that physicians do not understood her problem, that she will need hospitalization for the rest of her life, and that she may never live to fulfill her responsibilities to her family. Having tried medication that gave her no relief, she is convinced that to accept psychotherapy would be not only pointless but an admission of weakness.

A painstaking inquiry finally enables her to admit a life of unhappiness, regret, and impotent resentment. With great reluctance, she confesses that her unfulfilled life (in large part self-arranged) has left her afraid to plan for a normal future because she cannot risk any further disappointment. She nevertheless does not see her revelations as related to what she considers the *real* problem. Her fear of dying is based solely, as she sees it, on her physical condition. If that physical disorder could be cured, her other problems would be irrelevant, because, as she says, "I would continue to ignore them as I always have." Despite her painful admissions during the diagnostic interview, she cannot afford to see that her preoccupation with dying is a symptom. It is the price of wanting to retreat from adult life without taking conscious responsibility for the wish.

Here is an example of how mistaken efforts to maintain self-esteem undermine it still further. This patient's symptoms serve at least three purposes: they justify her retreat to a semi-invalid lifestyle, preserve her pride in being a conscientious mother, and punish her for her unconscious self-deception. The illness confesses an unacknowledged decision to sacrifice the truth of her existence for the sake of an unreal self-image. Selling her soul for the sake of that image keeps her a psychiatric cripple. Her disorder shows not only the power of anxiety to induce symbolic physical symptoms but, even more convincingly, the remarkable power exerted by the self-image or concept of self on which we depend to maintain our self-esteem.

The next case shows further how a lack of self-knowledge lays the groundwork for panic in people who have been insecure from an early age. Arthur, a high school graduate who was intellectually precocious but emotionally immature, planned to enter college in the fall. On a quiet summer afternoon, as he was idly browsing through the stacks of the local public library, he was suddenly alarmed by an unaccountably rapid pulse and the fear that he was suffering a heart attack. Although the reaction soon subsided, it left Arthur so preoccupied with his heart that any chance reference to that organ brought on another attack of panic. He went to college as planned, but the recurrent episodes were unrelieved by phenobarbital prescribed by a health service physician. Like other apprehensive patients of this type, Arthur was afraid to give the medication an adequate trial. The anxiety was so disturbing that he could not continue in school and dropped out for a semester.

Taken for consultation to a major clinic, Arthur had his first interview with a psychiatrist. The experience left him vaguely disappointed, with an instinctive sense that the interviewer had not really met him or understood the problem. Much more helpful was a cardiologist, who after a painstaking examination assured him that with his heart he would live a long time. The psychiatrist's superficial interview had failed to bring out significant information which the youth might have revealed if the interview had been conducted more skillfully. A secret and purely fantastic love interest had possessed him throughout his high school years. The girl was a fellow student with whom any realistic involvement was out of the question for Arthur, who was not only extremely shy but moved in a completely different social circle.

Only years later could Arthur begin to see how immersion in his fantasy had blinded him to the obvious adolescent handicaps of his social ineptness and immaturity. It was no coincidence that his panic appeared just as the idealized girl was to vanish from his world. Obsession with a hopeless love interest no longer made any sense, leaving him to go on with life as best he could. His anxiety episodes continued until rewarding friendships and academic accomplishment came to his rescue. It is worth observing, in this case as in so many others like it, that obsession with the heart (the symbol of love) carried an emotional meaning that was lost on the naive adolescent.

Diana, a bright college girl, repeatedly suffered acute anxiety about minor physical complaints which she took to be signs of serious or fatal illness. Medical reassurance gave her little more than temporary relief. Further inquiry revealed that she was also recurrently oppressed by moods of defeat and futility. She allowed work on her thesis to lapse until barely enough time remained to complete it. Only when reduced to helpless sobs by the feeling that all was lost could she bring herself to ask for help. She was beside herself with tension and embarrassment until straightforwardly confronted with the question of exactly what was keeping her from doing what was still possible. At first she could only protest that she did not know, but when asked whether an "I won't" might be present behind her "I can't," she finally confessed that her heart had never been in her studies. Although capable of superior work when she forced herself, she gained no satisfaction from such academic success as she achieved. Deeply uncertain about what she wanted to do with her life, she assumed it was her duty to be academically outstanding even though she had no real interest in the career for which she was ostensibly preparing.

Insecure throughout childhood and unsure of her goals, Diana alternated between two compensatory but contradictory modes of adaptation. Periods of overstriving for perfectionistic achievement were followed by humiliating lapses in responsibility when she allowed everything to slide. Her recurrent preoccupation with unrealistic fears about her health helped her ignore her contradictory motives, since a serious physical illness would free her from her halfhearted strivings without damaging her pride or confronting her with her unresolved ambivalence. She resorted to physical symptoms and fears, as so many people do, because physical illness is an eminently respectable defense. Even after she returned home with a degree, her unresolved tension culminated in episodes of impulsive rage. When anxiety cannot be relieved by one means, the desperate self finds another.

Elizabeth is a young woman whose longstanding anxiety leads to self-defeating behavior, chiefly compulsive in nature, based on her failure to confront or resolve her inner contradictions. At difficult times she also experiences episodes of shakiness, nausea, insomnia, and a sense of helplessness which she calls "hysterical." As a sensitive child, she had denied her own wishes and needs out of concern for a harried and over-burdened mother (at whom she later realized she was extremely angry). Finding it hard to say "no" or to "hurt" anyone, Elizabeth is now caught in a permanent vicious circle. Her excessive self-sacrifice creates resentment, her resentment creates a sense of guilt, and she must atone for her guilt by further self-sacrifice. Normal self-assertion is forbidden. In crises she somehow pulls herself together and does what the situation calls for, but only exceptionally can she act in her own interest. It finally dawns on her that she has the right to act on her own behalf only after an episode of anguished suffering lessens her sense of guilt. Her concern for her mother shows how she herself wants to be treated, but also hides her resentment of the mother's favoritism toward other siblings. Elizabeth feels cheated and envious because they got more recognition than she did. She finally admits that her heart is not in growing up but in getting what she missed as a child.

Her compulsive perfectionism is countered by a fear of responsibility that leads her to make errors. She purposely performs below her ability in hope that her school will dismiss her and relieve her from having to decide to quit on her own. Faced with an unavoidable situation not to her liking, she bursts out with "I can't take it." Here she is adopting weakness as a defense. It would be more honest for her to say, "It's not true that I can't take it. I don't *want* to take it. And because I have sacrificed myself for so long, I shouldn't *have* to take it. I'm sick of pleasing everyone at the cost of being a victim, but my resentment and guilt leave me no other choice."

Elizabeth accordingly feels entitled to a life in which she can win success without earning it and have her own way without offending anyone. She prefers to comfort herself by fantasizing that her problems are unreal or by blaming them on external conditions instead of taking responsibility upon herself. Although she repeatedly asks for advice on how to stop hating herself, she nevertheless continues her intellectualizing with no observable change in her behavior. In short, she generates her anxiety through a life of contradiction. She would rather claim weakness to evade a challenge than use her strength to meet it. Inwardly divided between compliance and resentment, she continues to invite failure through self-defeating ploys to avoid it. Her story illustrates how ambivalent family relations can become the nucleus of later problems.

The less we recognize our inner disunity, the more precarious our self-esteem and the more insecure our existence. Self-deception, however comforting at times, does not relieve us of responsibility for what we are doing with our lives. Yet the fraudulent dimension of anxiety is not something we consciously plan. The self that suffers anxiety must live with the consequences of its defensive strategy whether it foresaw them or not. It can overcome that anxiety only by swallowing false pride and confronting what it was formerly afraid to face.

Tom, a young physician in training, intelligent and knowledgeable, suffered acute anxiety when it was his turn to be on call. The anxiety was so intense while he was on duty that he feared he would have to abandon medicine as a career. As a small boy, he had reacted with tearful anxiety when separated from his mother, but the person most influential in his development was a demanding and critical father whom the boy admired but resented. Even while dependent on the mother, he grew to feel contempt for her, and thereafter his overriding motive was to prove that his father had judged him unfairly.

As a bright and attractive boy, Tom thrived on the approbation he won away from home, and he became more dependent on such accolades than he consciously realized. The need to create a superior impression required continuous comparison of himself with others. He had to present an outstanding image in all situations with a sustained demeanor of unruffled emotional control. This need led to his anxiety whenever he was on call. Not to come up with the immediate answer to every situation—merely having to ask someone else for help— would be a disastrous humiliation. Although he rapidly gained intellectual insight into the unrealistic nature of his expectations, he still needed time to master his tension when he was on call.

It is always difficult to reconcile one's personal version of reality with the world as others see it. The basic error, however, is not the failure to reach agreement with others, but the failure to be honest with oneself. To correct that dishonesty, one must undertake a humiliating correction of the self-image. Otherwise that image must continually defend itself against confronting a reality that refuses to disappear. In the two brief cases that follow, one person was able to face her true motives but the other one was not.

Norma, an intelligent and sensitive young woman, had always been so afraid of offending others that she was unable to be completely sincere, even with close friends. Guilt about her insincerity entailed anxiety, which she tried unsuccessfully to relieve by even further accommodation to other people. This vicious circle came to a head when a man persisted in pressing his unwelcome attentions on her. The resulting acute tension led Norma to seek psychotherapy, in which she came to face the futility of suppressing her true feelings. Successfully repelling the unwanted advances gave her enormous relief. As she finally understood the error of her pseudo-altruism, she triumphantly announced, "I am no longer lying to myself."

Olivia, a long-term victim of parental rejection, failed in everything she undertook. Subconsciously, her behavior was intended to punish her parents or at least make them regret their indifference to her. Long skilled at lying to herself, she regularly justified her recurrent failures by attributing them with questionable plausibility to external causes. Olivia's improbable excuses allowed her to hide the fact that *it was her own decision* to use failure as a form of retaliation. Her practiced self-deception also concealed the guilt that resulted from evading responsibility for her own decision. Although her strategy did not succeed in delivering her message to her parents, she was unable to give up her self-defeating behavior. To do so would have been to relinquish her unfulfilled need, and her pattern of living was so firmly entrenched that she could imagine no other way.

Chronic anxiety occurs in people who need immunity from any suffering or frustration. Without help, they can develop further defenses such as depression or obsessional behavior. Henry was an older man whose lifelong latent anxiety led to a series of errors in living that finally culminated in hospitalization for a severe state of depression. He at first felt completely unable to account for this development. In the course of a diagnostic interview, however, he recalled that his childhood had been a "disaster." As an insecure youth, Henry felt unable to live without the love of an ideal woman, even while he considered himself unworthy of one. Caught in that contradiction, he idealized unsuitable women, with the result that he was again and again disappointed in them and in himself. Shortly before his hospitalization, he suffered one more disappointment when he was rejected by a religious order (probably a mother symbol) where he had hoped to find peace at last. He concluded that he could not trust anyone, although in fact it was his own judgment that he could not trust. He had long lived on an intellectual plane divorced from his emotional reality. When that precarious system finally collapsed, he fell into a suicidal state that revealed his accumulated regrets and self-hatred. He dissolved in tears during the interview as he became aware of the sources of his depression: his suppressed anger and pain, his hopeless longing to start over as a child, and his shame about intense emotions incompatible with his self-image of detachment and control. There are two morals here: the first, that one gains no security through self-deception; the second, that living a secret life of disappointment and regret without adequate help can cause a disabling or even suicidal depression.

Some people abuse alcohol or drugs in their need to dull awareness of their anger at others and themselves. Walter, a man in his late thirties and a confirmed alcoholic since his teens, has struggled repeatedly but without success to give up drinking. His trial of several treatment programs has left him discouraged and disillusioned. After failed marriages and periods of success in business that were only temporary, he is at a loss to account for an apparent inability to tolerate success. He understands neither why he drinks nor why he relapses. All he knows is that he has been told alcoholism is a disease. During the interview, Walter looks depressed even while he denies any feeling of depression. He recalls, however, that throughout his childhood he always kept his indulgent parents unaware of his real feelings and his tendency to break rules. He has grown up concealing his emotions not only from everyone else but even from himself. Neither the programs that treated his "disease" nor the patient himself recognized the fact, which becomes strikingly evident in the interview, that even when he seemed most successful, he was living a life of self-deception and emotional pretense. He has escaped conscious anxiety by using alcohol to mask his unacknowledged depression. The meaning of his alcoholism finally becomes clear as a call for help with his failure to be true either to others or to himself.

The outcome is still unknown, but the conclusion is clear that one cannot live a lie without paying the price.

A paradoxical reaction appears in patients so anxiety-ridden that acting with self-respect (as if they were "normal") feels like a pretense they can no longer maintain. This consequence of profound anxiety is conspicuous in schizophrenics who resign themselves to a regressive existence. Restoring the self to a healthier level nevertheless need not be as onerous for others as it is for schizophrenics. With the right help, a self capable of growth learns to relinquish the defenses that blocked its development.

Some of these defenses deserve special mention. The need for an impossible degree of perfection keeps a person permanently insecure and dependent. Insisting on excessive entitlement or control leads to frustrated anger or depression. The need to dominate or disparage others entails fearing and distrusting them. In contrast, an exaggerated compulsion to please or placate others, whether prompted by fear or overidentification, finally ends in resenting them and despising oneself. But those who need to renounce intimacy altogether in order to forestall rejection create a different problem. They are compelled to live with a longing they can neither ignore nor fulfill.

Karen, a woman of great sensitivity, reports that her mind goes blank—she becomes mute and blocked—when she feels put on the spot by someone's unexpected disagreement or discourtesy. "It happens so fast that I have no control over it, and I don't have access to the feelings that I'm obliterating." Persuaded to report what she thinks at such moments, she says:

> Who am I to ask you to listen to me, to take up your time? I don't deserve to be taken seriously. I'm in the way. I feel you're wrong, but I don't have the right to even think this. The burden is on me to understand you, not vice versa. To have any connection with you, I've got to see the world on your terms. I don't have a right to define my own terms. I have been assuming that my whole existence is wrong. It's easier to be wrong than to fight back. If I fight back, you'll hate me. Then I might as well be dead. I need you to like me.

If you don't accept me or understand me, I'll be terribly alone. So I'll kill my own feelings. That way, I won't risk displeasing you. Of course, this is a bargain with the devil. If I sell my soul to have a connection with you, your connection is with an empty shell, not with me. If I'm not me, you will love the empty shell, not me. So I will still be lost and alone.

Karen's case demonstrates that self-sacrifice for the sake of acceptance merely increases a person's anxiety. Not only is the effort futile and unnecessary, but it arouses anger at the very people whose approval one craves.

Frank's episodes of acute anxiety occur when a habitual defense system suddenly proves unequal to the immediate situation. A man in his thirties with a tense and over-accommodating nature, Frank has always recoiled from unpleasant confrontations. Despite his efforts to get along with everyone, from time to time he suffers unexplained attacks of anxiety. The most recent of these occurred when an uncooperative fellow worker aroused more frustration than Frank could handle. The anxiety immediately followed a momentary surge of conscious anger to which he could give no expression at the time. He was later able to admit the anger in an interview with a therapist, but he was unable to make any sense of the anxiety that followed.

As an insecure child divided between the urge to attack and the fear of attack, Frank assumed that adversaries cannot assert their differences without destroying each other. He had therefore grown up trying to win approval through self-effacement. At the same time, he also bolstered his pride through gratifying a wholly unrecognized degree of self-will to which his self-effacement unconsciously entitled him. This double defense against his childhood anxiety entailed a problem he could not have foreseen. When the two defenses collided, which sooner or later they were bound to do, they created even greater anxiety. His self-sacrifice and self-will were not only at odds in principle, but they were ultimately handicaps, because in limiting his respect for himself and for his opponent, they made him incapable of healthy negotiation and further undermined his self-esteem. Even as he experienced his coworker as a threat and himself as a victim, he must have known at some level that he was no less hostile than his supposed adversary. Anxiety furthermore blocked his ability to empathize with his coworker or imagine why the man might have reason to behave in a way that Frank found so frustrating. His means of defense were bound to result in self-defeat.

When Frank's needs for control and appreciation were unexpectedly thwarted, the injury to his self-esteem provoked conscious anger. The anger in turn increased his anxiety because it clashed with his benevolent self-image. He had never suspected how much his self-esteem depended on getting his way in return for his compulsory self-effacement. His episode of anxiety therefore arose from the sudden unconscious realization that his defenses were in fact liabilities. Whenever his life situation required a degree of interpersonal maturity he had not yet attained, the inconsistency of his defenses could only add to his anxiety.

Autonomy is an intrinsic component of the psyche, and as such it is neither good nor bad. What matters is how it is expressed, for expressed it will be. Trying to abolish it only creates more pathology. In the form of healthy self-assertion, autonomy is guided by foresight and consideration for others. In excess, it becomes an egocentric form of self-will. People concerned with appearances usually suppress inappropriate forms of self-will, but in states of heightened anxiety, their unexpected impulsiveness can take both them and others by surprise. The indiscretions and offenses—aggressive, acquisitive, and sexual—that abound in public and private life testify to the power of unbridled self-will. Feelings of insecurity that lead to improper self-assertion can induce the pious to sin and permit agents of the law to violate what they are expected to defend.

Anxiety is not always clearly recognized as such, even when signs point to it, because many defenses serve to disguise it or limit its intensity. People often dismiss symptoms that they regard as inconsequential. It may be useful to consider a few of the author's own experiences of premonitory clues whose implications were not immediately apparent.

I once suffered a spell of tightness in the chest that came on without warning as I was giving a talk to students and staff. I found it difficult to speak and had to excuse myself in embarrassment. Returning to my apartment still in distress, I described my feelings to my wife as I sat beside her on a low, broad windowsill. As I talked, I spontaneously began to strike the sill with my fist, and as I pounded, I was astonished to feel an unexpected surge of anger replace the tension. I suddenly began to recall many occasions, some in childhood, in which a fear of disapproval forced me to suppress my anger. As I talked, I began to realize that my tension betrayed an unsuspected degree of resentment over insufficient recognition of my contribution. I was not yet ready to see that my demands for recognition were compensatory for a deeper level of anxiety whose existence I did not even suspect. Its sources and meaning would become evident only much later. At least I began to surmise the connection between my anxiety and unacknowledged aspects of my own personality, such as the hidden anger—and ultimately the passivity—that I had never before confronted.

Another learning experience. Driving down a busy street, I became furious with an aggressive driver. The intensity of my anger surprised me, and it took a while before I could ask myself what I was so angry about. As the anger subsided, I made an important discovery. I had grown up assuming that if I did what I had been taught was right, the other person was obligated to give me my way. I suddenly saw that I had no grounds for expecting the other driver to share my private assumptions. I also discovered that at a deeper level I envied the aggressiveness I had long ago been taught to renounce. This unacknowledged sense of entitlement also explained other occasions when frustration of my wishes evoked a surprising flare-up of anger. Getting my way was a hitherto unsuspected condition for maintaining my self-esteem. The failure of my unrealistic demand for control induced anxiety, and the anxiety had to be immediately concealed by compensatory anger.

In professional meetings, my impulse to speak up was sometimes checked by unexplained palpitations or tension in the chest. In time I discovered that what I really wanted was to demonstrate my superiority rather than contribute objectively to the issue at hand. This insight taught me to hold my peace until I knew what I was trying to do. Only then could I do what was required by the occasion and my role. This experience sheds light on the social phobias of people who suffer anxiety at the prospect of public scrutiny.

As I observed patients in staff interviews with others present, I sensed how reluctant they were to expose what they needed to hide, not only from strangers they were not ready to trust, but even from themselves. In time, the anxiety I felt in the course of my work alerted me to questionable motives of my own that I would once have overlooked, and I became aware of the frequently unrecognized role of anxiety in the lives of apparently normal people, not excluding those in the mental health professions.

Almost all the cases described so far illustrate defensive behavior of the kind usually labeled neurotic. There are also more seriously disturbed people who are unable to observe the usual requirements of convention. Some are simply too overwhelmed by their discordant emotions. Others cannot refrain from impulsive or short-sighted behavior in apparent disregard of the consequences.

Post-traumatic stress disorder, for example, arises from powerful feelings that the patient is unable to integrate. Many cases develop when military service thrusts young men and women into situations of unspeakable brutality for which they were never prepared. They are forced to suppress their natural feelings as they kill and witness killing. The loss of their buddies leaves them with the guilt of survivors who would rather have died instead. Full of intolerable shame, guilt and rage, they are torn between hatred for themselves and hatred for a world that ignores in practice what it preaches in public. At the same time, certain inhibited soldiers are shocked to find that killing gives them a sense of power they have never known before. On returning home, they are caught between accepting the requirements of peacetime society and giving vent to their feelings of murderous rage.

Lionel, one such veteran, felt he no longer deserved the love he yearned for, nor could he risk intimacy in any case, because he could not tolerate the possibility of disappointment. Suffering intense flash-backs and unwilling to share his ordeals with people he felt could never understand, he lived in isolation until loneliness drove him back into society. In a veterans' hospital, he found partial relief in meeting other veterans with whom he could at least feel some kinship.

There are many people who cannot bring themselves to live by the rules of the law-abiding world. Antisocial characters are an out-standing example. At an early age, they adopt an impulsive lifestyle with an urge to defy authority. Self-contempt and despair of the future underlie a lack of foresight that seems incongruent with their intelli-gence. Having abandoned hope of legitimate success, they settle for transient triumphs of self-will. If they get away with their rash behavior, they enjoy a temporary sense of power. If they don't get away with it, they find relief in having an authority take charge of their lives. While apparently asserting their autonomy, they are discharging their rage yet unconsciously pursuing the security gained through sub-mission to punishment and control. In such cases, whose motivation baffles a naively punitive legal system, imprisonment and even the threat of execution cannot be counted on to deter crime.

Recurrent cycles of self-will and self-blame reveal the anger and guilt, usually long accumulated, that govern people who have failed to develop a constructive way of life. When such cycles persist into adult life, they are unconscious pleas for the empathic understanding and discipline that as children they never received. Pathological expres-sions of self-will need not be the work of an untamable id; they can be defenses against anxiety by asserting the "me." This strategy is less socially acceptable than seeking reassurance through the "you," but it may be irresistible to a self that feels validated by the exercise of power. When self-will and the need for approval are mobilized with equal but opposite force, the collision can be dramatic. For example, girls with anorexia or bulimia, who feel helplessly caught between the need to conform and the need to defy, hang on to their symptoms as their only means of asserting autonomy, no matter how much shame they may suffer in the process.

Psychological symptoms are indirect confessions. They provide unconscious relief even when attended by conscious humiliation, because they are pleas for help with problems the self is unable to solve. Consider affronts to self-regard, from which no one is entirely safe. An unrealistic insistence on psychological immunity to any affront is asking for trouble. We handle insults best when we are secure enough to treat them with undefensive composure. Otherwise we remain vulnerable to everything that offends our pride.

All distortions and denials of reality are consequential decisions. People who make such decisions cheat themselves of what they could have been. A vulnerable self-image keeps them hypersensitive to criticism, prone to errors of judgment, and quick to denigrate others as well as themselves. Such impaired interpersonal competence reduces a person's success in life, further reinforcing any preexisting sense of inferiority.

Anxiety is not a purely private matter. Others are involved in its origin, its expression, and its results. Some susceptibility to anxiety is probably unavoidable, because the self-image, which controls our response to others, is seldom perfectly accurate. But if the self is too insecure, that image may need to be maintained at the cost of self-deception.

To be truly secure, one must first be true to oneself, something the wise have always known. As Rabbi Zusya of Hanipol (d. 1800) neared the end of his days, he told his disciples, "When I arrive in the world to come, they will not ask me, 'Why were you not Moses?' They will ask me, 'Why were you not Zusya?'"

TO SOMEONE
CONSIDERING
PSYCHOTHERAPY

Psychotherapy is a guided adventure in taking responsibility—not for the person you think you are, but for the person you are. The outcome depends on how well your self-image ultimately matches your reality, or in Sullivan's words, to what extent "the patient as known to himself is much the same as the patient behaving with others." The aim of psychotherapy is therefore to help you face what you are really doing with your life.

Sometimes disparaged and sometimes overvalued, psychotherapy in some form has been practiced since antiquity. Troubled people have always needed to turn to others for help when their own resources were inadequate. But not everything that goes by the name of psychotherapy is therapeutic. Some would-be practitioners of the art are too limited to provide real help. Typical of such incompetence was a therapist who frightened her impressionable patient into panic by rashly suggesting that her father had molested her. That therapist was wrong. With the help of an experienced therapist, the patient went on to a healthy life.

Psychotherapy is not a science and is not likely to become one. It is an experiment in which you and your therapist collaborate to increase the competence in living that comes with accurate self-knowledge. Finding the right therapist may take time and repeated trials. What matters is not the therapist's reputation or professional degrees, but what you learn as you work together. Never hesitate to voice your questions and doubts as they occur to you, and then make sure you are being understood and taken seriously. You are not there to please the therapist but to learn how to act in your own behalf. Good therapists are responsible for their own self-esteem and do not rely on their patients for reassurance; they know their first responsibility is to you. In meeting that obligation, they need to be aware of every shift in your emotional state, especially in your level of anxiety.

Honesty is called for on the part of both therapist and patient. Giving the therapist false or incomplete information wastes your time, not to speak of your money. Nor is psychotherapy a time for agreeable conversation. If you feel no tension or discomfort in the course of therapy, you are evading the real problems. Your aim is to face what you are doing that is against your own interest, and to endure the necessary anxiety that is part of the process.

Therapy is not something that another person does *to* you or *for* you, the way physicians perform surgery or prescribe medication. You are in therapy to increase your mastery of your innate resources, not to have an expert make your decisions or direct your life. In any case, what you accomplish is up to you, for you will get only where you want to go. If you feel you are not being helped, you must say so without apology. Sir William Osler (1849–1919) perceptively observed that what kind of patient has the disease is more important than what kind of disease the patient has. This observation is eminently true in psychotherapy.

You or your therapist may be eager to try medication, but care must be taken not to resort to medication prematurely, so as to avoid the risk of suppressing your anxiety before you understand what it means. While it naturally makes sense to relieve symptoms as soon as possible, the deeper message of the anxiety must never be ignored and should not be postponed. It may mean that you are not facing what you cannot afford to overlook, or it warns you to reconsider an action that is premature or unwise. Undefensively accepting what you really are ensures your emotional security. While drugs sometimes provide symptom relief, they pose the risk of dependency while helping you evade critical issues. Even though certain antidepressants sometimes relieve panic states, it is best to reserve medication for anxiety of incapacitating nature.

A therapeutic group experience teaches you that others have troubles like yours and helps you become more objective about yourself. If you fear exposure to a group, further therapy may help you overcome your fear of being seen as others see you.

You must meet every trial as best you can. If you feel anxiety on an airplane trip but have the courage to keep flying, the nervous system will finally adapt, and the tension will subside. Don't condemn yourself because you suffer anxiety and don't worry about what others think. Anxiety is not a reason for shame but a reaction to be understood and mastered; unnecessary shame further undermines your already damaged self-regard.

Don't try to explain or justify your problems by finding fault with yourself or anyone else. When you make mistakes, as we all do, view them as opportunities to learn, not as signs of inferiority or reasons to punish yourself. Your humiliating experiences can teach you where you have based your self-esteem on mistaken assumptions. If a feeling of anxiety comes out of the blue, ask yourself what you are doing—or are tempted to do—that could lead to regret. Reassuring talk or measuring yourself against others rarely helps. Self-esteem grows through living with respect for yourself and for others. If you are trapped in a self-destructive system of living, which is often based on long-standing anger at oneself and others, you must make a strenuous effort to give up the defenses you thought you could not live without.

Psychotherapy can be invaluable if you are entrapped in a self-defeating way of life, but it is not always available on demand. If left to your own resources, you will find it useful to question yourself along lines such as: What am I feeling? What do I really want? What is in my real interest? Whose disapproval do I fear? What outcome must I avoid? Can I act on a decision and learn from the result? If an interpretation disturbs me, can I look at the evidence and explain my reaction?

Never ignore your intuitions or marginal thoughts, because they arise from an otherwise untapped source of insight. In critical situations where you feel unprepared for the reality confronting you, these messages from the unconscious are especially significant. Each time you face up to what you previously feared, you achieve greater self-respect and control over your life. But mere intellectual understanding is not enough. Insights should be put to the test in daily living. This may require self-assertion where you once might have been afraid to speak up, or it may even require silence where your first impulse is to speak unwisely.

Shakespeare gave the last word to old Polonius, who advised his son Laertes:

> This above all: to thine own self be true,
> And it must follow as the night the day,
> Thou canst not then be false to any man.
> *Hamlet*, Act I, scene 3

THE SINNER
IN THE SAINT

A Psychological Note
on Saint Teresa of Avila

S aint Teresa of Avila was a gifted and determined woman who suffered symptoms that today would be seen as pathological. Yet in her life and work she creatively transcended her symptoms, intuitively integrating their unconscious significance with her religious faith and turning them in this way to constructive ends. Her accomplishment was evidently not attained without paying an almost fatal price. Every choice of a single-minded way of life means the renunciation of all other potentialities, and such renunciation may be agonizing and even dangerous when some vital demand has to be denied. Saint Teresa's life is a reminder that whatever the problem a person faces, one should never underestimate the quality of that person's character. It can be a decisive factor, at times capable of surmounting inner dilemmas that at first seem irreconcilable.

It is hard to resist a smile when the good Saint Teresa (1515–1582) proclaims her wickedness in the very first sentence of her autobiography (*The Life of Teresa of Jesus: The Autobiography of Teresa of Avila*). What kind of person is this, whose life of dedication to her faith is accompanied by constant self-disparagement? All this in the face of her determined self-discipline, her respect for her superiors, and her energetic contribution to her church and her order. In Saint Augustine

(353–430) we see a comparable self-deprecation. To common sense, this attitude seems extreme and oddly inappropriate, but for the honest sinner it marks an acute self-appraisal that confesses an inability to attain the perfection that the spirit pursues. Personalities of this type suffer from the complexity of their natures and the impossibility of ever becoming a completely spiritual being. The endless exertions of Saint Teresa in this direction entail a constant dissatisfaction with mortal limitations and consequent preoccupation with a "wickedness" that paradoxically expresses an inextinguishable obsession with virtue.

Saint Teresa grew up in the Catholic world of renaissance Spain and found in its terms and practices the proper outer garment for her inner life—proper but hardly easy or painless. To express her sense that some element intrinsic to her nature resisted her ideal, Saint Teresa wrote in her incisive manner, "Anything good in me was not mine at all." She could not forgive herself, because she was "vain and liked to be well thought of in the things wont to be esteemed by the world." She seriously strove to repudiate vanity and social esteem. However, she seemed not to recognize that despite striving for the humility required by her faith, she had not yet relinquished her need for approval. She was merely sacrificing the approval of the world at large for the approval of her own specialized community.

The lives of even the most capable persons can be complicated by assumptions that they dare not question. The fear of acknowledging one's forbidden motives always plays a part in generating anxiety and must have contributed to Saint Teresa's difficulties. The language and concepts are those of Catholic Spain, but the human predicament is universal. Her terror of "attachments" (her term for the devils against whom she defends herself) must be understood as a fear of promptings contrary to her spiritual ideal. How to be rightly attached and rightly unattached to a contradictory world has always been the problem of the virtuous and the wise; it reappears in every great religion.

In Saint Teresa's case, the signs of internal strain took a physical form, and she describes at length "the numerous infirmities which His Majesty began to send" her. These included fainting fits, heart trouble, episodes of unconsciousness, fever, and "nervous pains." Although these disorders were probably aggravated by the well-meant but ignorant ministrations of the time, the variety, duration, and character of the ailments strongly suggest a psychological component in their origin. If this is so, these dramatic attacks of illness bear witness to the life struggle of this young, intense, and sensitive woman, gripped by a profound urge to transcend a part of herself in order to fulfill the spiritual ideals of her world, ideals that the multitude may acknowledge but only a few take completely and literally to heart. Her illness was experienced as a visitation, a test that came from God as the power who required a supreme spiritual sacrifice, the effort to wrestle a renounced but inalienable part of her nature into submission.

It is probably not a matter of chance that similar disorders marked the careers of two other women who also emerged from a sickly adolescence, troubled by psychosomatic or hysterical symptoms, to become leaders in religious movements. I am referring to Mary Baker Eddy (1821–1910) and to Ellen G. White (1827–1915). This interpretation should not be taken as derogatory. It recognizes the real physical cost that is wrung even from exceptionally gifted people who strive to overrule basic aspects of their nature in the effort to fulfill a socially inculcated ideal.

The following passage is a telling example of the Saint's self-analysis:

I also fell victim to another excess of zeal, which was to beseech God, and to make it my special prayer, that when a person thought there was any good in me, His Majesty would reveal my sins to him, so that he might see how utterly undeserving I was of those favors—which is always my great desire. My confessor told me not to do this, but I continued to do it almost down to this day. If I observed that someone was thinking well of me, I would manage, indirectly or in any way that I could, to make him aware of my sins. That seemed to bring me relief. My sins have made me very scrupulous about this. This, however, I think, was not the result of humility, but often proceeded from a temptation. It seemed to me that I was deceiving everybody; and, though it is true that it was their own belief that there was some good in me which was deceiving them, I had no desire to deceive them, nor did I ever try to do so; for some reason the Lord permitted it. So, unless I saw that such a course was necessary, I said nothing about these things even to my confessors, for to do so would have caused me grave scruples. I realize now that all these little fears and troubles and this apparent humility were sheer imperfection, due to my lack of mortification. For a soul left in the hands of God cares nothing whether good or evil is spoken of it if it has a right understanding.

The Life of Teresa of Jesus

Note the comfort Saint Teresa derives from ascribing to the Lord that which she herself cannot understand or control, very much as people nowadays breathe with a sense of relief once they recognize the futility of trying to understand and control everything themselves. The Saint had the advantage of relying on the ultimate benevolence of a divine power that transcended her comprehension.

One cannot justly quarrel with Saint Teresa's understanding of herself, which was ultimately adequate for her life work. Whether psychoanalytic therapy would have made a positive difference in her career is a topic for idle speculation. One kind of self-analysis and self-healing was nevertheless available to the determined Saint, and that was prayer.

The enormous investment of her energy in the experience and meaning of prayer pervades all of Saint Teresa's writings. The stages and struggles of prayer occupied her continuous and passionate attention. She reported them with endless patience and in nuanced detail. The time and effort she devoted to prayer served not only to guide the Saint in her life decisions but also to mitigate much of the anxiety generated by her chosen way of life. The guilt-relieving effect of the suffering that went with her search for self-abnegation comes to clear expression in this statement:

No words will suffice to describe the way in which God wounds the soul and the sore distress which He causes it, so that it hardly knows what it is doing. Yet so delectable is this distress that life holds no delight which can give greater satisfaction. As I have said, the soul would gladly be dying of this ill.

The soul that suffers because of its human limitations longs to burst its bounds and transcend them, yet it can exist as a conscious spirit only because of them. It is this paradox that religion, and mystical experience in particular, tries to resolve or escape. The matter is put with moving fervor by San Juan de la Cruz (St. John of the Cross) in the following poem:

> *Vivo sin vivir en mí*
> *Y de tal manera espero*
> *Que muero porque no muero.*
>
> I live without living in myself
> And my hope is such
> That I die because I am not dying.
> > *Coplas del alma que pena por ver a Dios*
> > (Songs of the soul that suffers to see God)

Saint Teresa uses this triplet to introduce a poem of her own that repeats the last line as its refrain and again expresses the desire to lose her life in order to gain it, echoing, of course, the words of Jesus: "And he that loseth his life for my sake shall find it" (Matthew 10:39).

Finally we come to the Saint's visions, experiences that caused both her and her advisers considerable concern before their source could be correctly ascertained and their validity could receive the imprimatur. For today's psychologist, it is not so pressing a matter to determine whether God or the devil is the source of such visions. Basically a sensible and practical soul, Saint Teresa did not occupy herself with such vexing questions as how the devil and the Lord transact their affairs. To the great convenience of the psychoanalyst, they both seem to operate a good deal of the time in the unconscious.

It may surprise some people to learn that visions and hallucinations are not *prima facie* symptoms of mental disorder. The current culture discourages and undervalues such messages from the unconscious, but they are as significant and potentially instructive as dreams, of which they are a waking equivalent. In serious forms of mental disorder, hallucinations are a sign that one can no longer experience oneself as a psychologically unified person. If, however, the psyche is more secure and integrated, intuiting the significance of those symptoms enlarges the range and depth of one's self-understanding. The conflicting modes of defense that underlie anxiety are open to compromise or reconciliation in many ways, not always negative.

Such was the case with Saint Teresa. Her visions helped sustain her psychic equilibrium in the presence of strong conflictual forces. All her life she struggled to surmount the contest between what she felt was her inner good and her inner evil. But in time she was able to accept both. The evil element formed her terrifying vision of hell. The good element inspired her ecstatic vision of Christ, the symbol of such love and life as she physically relinquished but spiritually attained.

Here is a person whose inner life outweighed everything else, yet whose character required interaction with a world whose constant demands she felt obligated to meet. Through the stress of this existence, her visions maintained her balance. Her deepest instinct spoke in the words, "Everything I see is like a dream, and what I see with my bodily eyes is a mockery." If she had been a more conventional spirit, she might have needed no visions, but neither would she have tested the strength of her soul in its human effort to scale the celestial mount.

Although she was troubled by physical and emotional pathology, Saint Teresa's experience shows that it is possible to exploit even error and illusion in a fashion that gives them value. In a sympathetic religious context, the Saint's responses to her difficulties are usually accepted without question. Such responses might be questioned by a contemporary psychiatrist, yet they not only permitted but may even have contributed to a healthy outcome. Such a result might be difficult to accomplish without a supportive milieu and the determination of an exceptional personality, but the Saint's achievement shows us there is never only one right way to live a fulfilled life in this confusing world.

PART TWO

OUR INCOHERENT
WORLD

Die Erde war zu lange schon ein Irrenhaus!
(The Earth been a lunatic asylum for too long.)
Nietzsche, *On the Genealogy of Morals*, Second Essay

The human race has a long and imperfectly understood history, recently explored by Jared Diamond in his pioneering volume, *Guns, Germs and Steel*. This work shows us that natural environments are important in determining the success or failure of various civilizations throughout history. What Diamond does not address is man's internal environment, his inborn psychological makeup. When there is competition for resources, why do human societies resort to aggression rather than negotiation? To answer such questions, we cannot ignore the human personality. The scope of individual behavior may be limited but is never insignificant, for all history is the cumulative outcome of individual decisions. But even more to the point, the distinctive attributes of the human mind must have societal as well as individual consequences. It is therefore worth exploring the probability that humankind complicates its social problems by resorting collectively to defensive behavior.

We have already mentioned the biological contribution to our difficulties. The imperfect integration of different levels of the human brain makes it difficult for us to coordinate our capacity for reason with the intensity of our emotions. Under duress, the psyche attempts to reduce emotional distress by restricting the range of conscious experience. What is too difficult to assimilate consciously is relegated to a less accessible level of the nervous system. The result is a state of psychic disunity that allows an instinctive response to bypass the use of reason. While this disunity may be valuable in a life-threatening crisis, it causes problems in situations where we have time to analyze yet fail to consider the deeper motives or consequences of our behavior.

Almost everyone resorts to some form of defensive behavior in the course of social interaction. Our discussion of anxiety has described how repression of unacceptable motives leads a person to create a false self. One engages in defensive behavior to protect this self-image from evaluation, either by oneself or others. This behavior is considered *defensive* because one reacts as if his identity (his right to be himself) is under threat, even if in reality the threat is only to the false self-image.

Governments, whose primary concern is power, engage in deception that is often deliberate. While leaders like to proclaim such respectable motives as serving the public, solving the nation's problems, and promoting peace, they are much less ready to admit the desire to expand their power, control the distribution of resources, or limit dissent. Neither autocratic nor democratic regimes publicly admit to all of their real motives. To put it more bluntly, as the late investigative journalist I. F. Stone said, "All governments lie."

Governments are like individuals in their need to maintain pride, deny errors, and pursue conflicting goals. When a government faces a threat, whether real or perceived, an intelligent response requires an objective assessment of the entire situation. But when the need to hide the truth is stronger than the need to cope honestly with a problem, the government becomes defensive. It may then institute political repression, engage in secret illegal activity, or resort to armed aggression.

To a government unwilling to deal with problems openly, diplomacy can be perceived as a greater danger than war. The prospect of making concessions or revealing secrets is not tolerated by a government intent on preserving its position at any cost. War is therefore avoidance rather than engagement of the essential issues. In the absence of frank communication, neither party can achieve a clear understanding of the other's aims. Defensiveness and distrust mount on both sides, and it is impossible to reach a resolution. The parallel to individual defensiveness is evident. The decision to go to war is undertaken as an effort to relieve insecurity, but it serves instead to increase it. Anyone who believes an international crisis can be solved by war soon learns that the reality of war is far worse than the crisis it was meant to solve.

A government needs the support of its citizens if it is to wage war. It is ordinary citizens, not the leaders, who will be subjected to violence, injury, or death. Then how does a government convince people to support a policy which is obviously against their true interest? After World War II, the psychologist G. M. Gilbert asked Hermann Göring, Hitler's second in command, how Hitler was able to mobilize his people for a war of aggression. Göring's answer proves instructive:

Göring: Why, of course, the people don't want war. Why would some poor slob on a farm want to risk his life in a war when the best that he can get out of it is to come back to his farm in one piece? Naturally, the common people don't want war; neither in Russia nor in England nor in America, nor for that matter in Germany. That is understood. But, after all, it is the leaders of the country who determine the policy and it is always a simple matter to drag the people along, whether it is a democracy or a fascist dictatorship or a Parliament or a Communist dictatorship.

Gilbert: There is one difference. In a democracy, the people have some say in the matter through their elected representatives, and in the United States only Congress can declare wars.

Göring: Voice or no voice, the people can always be brought to the bidding of the leaders. That is easy. All you have to do is tell them they are being attacked and denounce the pacifists for lack of patriotism and exposing the country to danger. It works the same way in any country.

G. M. Gilbert, *Nuremberg Diary*

Political leaders create fear by using carefully crafted propaganda, half-truths, and innuendo. Such measures convinced Americans in 2003 that Iraq posed an imminent threat to their safety. When this premise was disproved, the government produced further rationales. George Orwell warned us how governments manipulate language, but many Americans evidently accepted the Orwellian declarations that fighting in Iraq would bring peace, freedom, and democracy to the Middle East.

Ideally, an informed public should be able to distinguish war propaganda from valid argument. But conditions of fear and insecurity have an infantilizing effect on many people. Instead of thinking for themselves, they prefer to leave decisions to a powerful and protective authority. When insecurity and gullibility infect the press too, few of us can reach an objective appraisal of reality.

War stirs up prejudice and racism. Military training dehumanizes the enemy in order to encourage soldiers to kill. On the home front, people become suspicious of anyone who looks like the enemy. The menace of racial stereotyping was illustrated in the days after September 11, 2001, by the murder of a Sikh in Arizona. The innocent victim's turban reminded a confused, angry man of Osama bin Laden.

Modern military technologies make it possible to kill without witnessing the gruesome reality of killing. It is easier to kill a person one does not see face to face. It is also easier to kill the wrong people— not only innocent civilians but even one's allies. (For these deadly mistakes, governments invent such sanitizing terms as *collateral damage* and *friendly fire*.) Even many decades after hostilities have ceased, landmines continue killing and maiming innocent civilians, including children.

One sometimes hears that World War II was a "good" war, that it was justified by the dangers of fascism. Howard Zinn, a historian and World War II veteran, makes the point that there is no such thing as a good war because "war poisons everybody." We are familiar with the atrocities of Hitler, but we forget that the United States also committed atrocities. In the atomic bombing of Hiroshima and Nagasaki and the firebombing of Dresden and Tokyo, the United States was responsible for hundreds of thousands of civilian deaths. When an enemy kills noncombatants on this scale, we call it a war crime.

Only in war is it possible to rationalize such crimes as killing civilians or torturing captives. The polar opposites "us and them" become subtly equivalent to another set of opposites, "good and evil." The unconscious pseudologic goes something like this:

(1) *We* are good.
(2) Since *they* are our enemy, they are evil.
(3) If evil is eliminated, only good will remain.
(4) We are justified in using any means to defend the good.
(5) We therefore are entitled to kill our enemy.

Such thinking allows us to do exactly what we condemn in our enemy, and blinds us to our own inhumanity and the humanity of our adversaries. The idea that one can destroy evil by killing someone is a fallacious but persistent myth. Killing corrupts the killer and arouses hatred and revenge in the opponent, escalating a cycle of violence.

The human cost of war is irreparable. The monetary cost is also a human cost. The government of the United States spends billions of dollars on the military and claims it cannot afford universal healthcare for its citizens. Funds devoted to humanitarian aid and international cooperation amount to a mere fraction of what we spend on weapons and war. While our government uses the word *security* to imply that war protects us, one can argue that we would feel far safer if we had adequate healthcare and could send our children to college instead of the battlefield.

Sooner or later it will be necessary to forgo the millennial resort to armed conflict by imposing limits on national sovereignty. This will be extremely difficult to put into effect, for nations stubbornly insist on their sovereignty as an absolute right. Woodrow Wilson's League of Nations was an utter failure. Its successor, the United Nations, is currently active but devitalized by the disproportionate power of a few favored nations. The prospect for a less violent world therefore remains dim, yet change becomes more imperative than ever with the growth of world population and the increasing risk that irresponsible parties will acquire nuclear weapons.

On the domestic front, we implement many policies that do not stand up to logical scrutiny. For example, capital punishment is justified as a means of preventing crime and administering appropriate justice, but it also serves less rational motives. Many district attorneys and judges, whose jobs depend on public approval and elections, want to show they are "tough on crime." Their commitment to justice is sometimes outweighed by the desire to bolster their careers. Police investigators are under pressure to solve criminal cases with dispatch; they sometimes focus prematurely on the wrong suspect, excluding other possibilities and at times even suppressing exculpatory evidence. Attorneys sometimes use tainted evidence and other dubious tactics when their overriding goal is not to discover the truth but to win the case. And finally, the refusal of police, attorneys, judges, or politicians to admit their errors plays a significant role throughout the criminal justice system, even when lives are at stake.

In the courtroom, it is not easy for a jury to disentangle the facts of a case from the web of motives underlying the arguments. Attorneys are skilled at arousing sympathy for a victim or evoking horror over the nature of a crime. Their aim is to distract the jury from its responsibility to be convinced of the facts beyond a reasonable doubt. A jury may then deliver a conviction based on emotion rather than evidence and logic.

Human beings harbor such a deep and primitive urge for vengeance that often little else matters. The urge to kill a murderer seems to spring from the expectation that the murderer's death will expunge the evil that has been done. But no act of vengeance or justice can restore the victim to life. Capital punishment therefore cannot bring closure to the victim's family, whose loss is permanent and irremediable. Executing the murderer merely creates a second victim and a second grieving family. And if the defendant is innocent but found guilty, he may have to sacrifice his life for a flawed system. The community is harmed as well, since the unidentified perpetrator may remain at large and continue to pose a threat.

Capital punishment is legally authorized murder, and it compromises the morality of government. Despite our self-image as a civilized society dedicated to justice and the rule of law, our ideals fall prey to excessive personal ambition, insufficient concern for our fellow beings, and reluctance to admit our mistakes. In our haste to condemn the sinner, we forget his humanity and overlook our own sins. But the most flagrant contradiction is the hardest to face: in killing a murderer, we are not eliminating sin but committing the very sin that we aim to eradicate.

Many other policies or positions are motivated by considerations other than our stated ideals. Here we can offer only a few brief examples:

- We refuse to limit the proliferation of guns in our society. People justify their opposition to gun control by appealing to freedom, but no society needs the kind of freedom that makes it easier for its citizens to kill one another. The real issue is whether weapons manufacturers should be free to earn their profits at the expense of public safety.

- Current efforts to dismantle Affirmative Action are gaining popularity even though serious inequities remain in our society. A color-blind society is a worthy goal, but recently this phrase is used as a covert means of slowing the progress of integration while paying lip service to equality.

- Legislative initiatives regarding such personal matters as sexual conduct and abortion claim to be motivated by concern for our moral values, but their real aim may be to divert public attention from such critical issues as the maldistribution of wealth and power.

- There is worldwide agreement among scientists about the contribution of human activity to global warming. Yet industries hire their own experts to contradict the professional consensus, and the United States censors government scientists who reach conclusions unfavorable to government policy. In shielding industry from responsibility to control emissions, the United States protects corporate profits while endangering the future of the planet.

Politicians have become extremely sophisticated in promoting policies that cater to special interests rather than the public's needs. By clever use of language and by limiting access to critical information, they manipulate public discourse and conceal their real intentions. Now it is time for the public to become more sophisticated in interpreting political rhetoric. Until the public understands the real motives behind government propaganda, it will continue to be fooled into supporting policies against its best interest. In his *Outline of History*, H. G. Wells summarized the essence of our predicament in a single sentence: "Human history becomes more and more a race between education and catastrophe." The outcome of this race is far from certain.

THE CONTRIBUTION
OF SCIENCE

For is it not possible that science as we know it today, or a "search for the truth" in the style of traditional philosophy, will create a monster?

Paul Feyerabend, *Against Method*

Most people have only a superficial grasp of science and the complex data it has assembled, but they still are impressed by what science has given us in the form of knowledge of the physical world, technological progress, and the treatment of disease. What matters in the present context, though, is where science has brought us as a civilization.

Science has made enormous progress not only in enhancing human life but in destroying it. Nuclear bombs and other lethal weapons now make war more dangerous for civilians than for soldiers in arms. Modern industrial processes pollute land, water, and air. Our supermarkets are stocked with artificial and processed foods that look appealing and have a long shelf life, but carry little nutritive value and sometimes threaten our health. The responsibility for such problems does not rest exclusively with scientists. It also rests with the misuse of science by human beings whose primary motives are power and greed.

Scientists have become a contemporary guild of isolated specialists, for their activities and concerns are barely understood or shared by the rest of the world. In its state of semi-isolation, the scientific enterprise illustrates the lack of integration that is characteristic of our time. This state of affairs has undoubtedly arisen from the highly technical education that enables scientists and theorists to do their work. But the fact that most people remain naive and sometimes gullible in the field of science does nothing to ensure that scientific progress will benefit society as a whole. It merely makes it easier for those who profit from scientific findings to take advantage of humanity's widespread ignorance and gullibility.

Despite their claims of objectivity and rationality, scientists are human beings with their own motives and often hidden agendas. In science and medicine, as in all areas of culture, ideas go in and out of style. One should not assume that something is true just because some expert says so. Science can be politicized when those in power want to limit research in such fields as stem cell research, promote wasteful programs such as military space technologies, or offer biased opinions in matters such as global warming. There are a few unscrupulous members of the scientific community who are willing to promulgate erroneous data or theories in order to support the agendas of those who pay their salaries. Most scientists honor their responsibility to serve the public good, but their views are sometimes ignored by the policy makers in power. One thinks immediately of J. Robert Oppenheimer and other prominent physicists who advised against developing the hydrogen bomb.

The effectiveness of advertising and the limited judgment of buyers play a conspicuous part in how scientific advances are delivered to the American people. Pharmaceutical corporations show more interest in their sales than in the uncertain benefits of many novel products. In order to increase profits, they market newer and supposedly better medications and medical technologies, without sufficient proof of their safety or effectiveness. Aggressive marketing to both doctors and patients puts pressure on the entire healthcare system to adopt increasingly expensive treatments, even when their safety or therapeutic value have not been sufficiently demonstrated. Some medications and surgical procedures have long been accepted as standards of care before they are found to be untherapeutic or even harmful. The use of lobotomy to treat intractable psychosis is one example.

Scientific innovations in agriculture introduce other social problems. The development of genetically engineered crops, justified as an effort to reduce world hunger, enriches agribusiness but has increased poverty among poor rural farmers. To make use of such technology, farmers must now purchase seeds from multinational corporations instead of following their age-old tradition of saving seeds from one harvest to the next. Burdened by the high costs of the new technologies, the disaster of drought, and the shame of overwhelming debt, an unprecedented number of poor Indian cotton farmers have been driven to suicide.

Yet politicians, who are chiefly concerned with reelection, are loath to challenge the groups that give them financial support. Many policy makers accept or reject scientific advice because of its political or religious implications instead of basing their decisions on objective data. The average person thus survives at the mercy of disparate interests that disregard the needs of the community at large.

Given the human limitations of those in the field of science as well as those invested financially in its products, one can hardly rely on science to solve the problems of society. The scientific contribution to human welfare, valuable as it may be, does not relieve us of the need to look for the unacknowledged motives of those who claim to act in the interest of mankind.

MAKING SENSE
OF EXPERIENCE

MEANING

*M*eaning is a protean word. It can refer to anything that a conscious being might experience or enact. One can distinguish two fundamental levels of meaning. The primary level is the *self-evident* as such, our immediate sense perceptions as distinct from the information they convey. The second level is *what the self-evident implies*. The nature of the first level is undeniable; the second level can always be questioned or revised.

Meaning pervades all experience. As *value* (what makes life worth living), meaning is at the heart of our existence. As *purpose*, meaning is the basis on which we understand the behavior of living things and order our lives. As *intention*, it refers to the pursuit of a specific goal. It can also apply to an end state that will compensate for earlier unfulfillment. As *prediction*, meaning is the mainstay of our survival. In going beyond the immediately given, meaning has no assurance of being correct. We learn the probable import of our primary data through unavoidable inference and speculation.

Primary meaning is what remains when interpretation is suspended or unnecessary. Such would be the unmistakable sound of thunder, the scent of a rose, the color of the sky, or a self-evident insight. Secondary meaning is derived from the self-evident through a process of interpretation or prediction. The thunder announces a storm. Letters on a page form words that tell a story. The chiming of a clock announces the hour. The baby's whimper lets us know it is time for a diaper change. All such conclusions are provisional and subject to error. They are hypotheses, not certainties, and cannot be taken as true without further confirmation. Truth, the complete description of how things really are, is a conceptual ideal, constantly pursued but never completely attainable.

Interpretation, the process of decoding a message, is the servant of meaning. Messages need to be interpreted correctly in the light of their context, but their interpretation, which always involves an element of uncertainty, can never be entirely free from the interpreter's bias. Senders are responsible for the message they send, but only in part for how it will be received. Misunderstandings are unavoidable. Even the literate and intelligent are limited by their assumptions, and they too are capable of misinterpreting and criticizing before they have completely grasped what they have just read or heard.

Some thinkers view *interpretation* as subjective, *explanation* as objective. In a scientific context, explanation implies intersubjective agreement, a consensus about the data that support or refute a given hypothesis. Interpretation, on the other hand, depends on one's subjective, though not necessarily arbitrary, identification with the mind of another person. When we read Shakespeare, we talk to ourselves in Shakespeare's words, but it is we who decide what his words mean. One cannot automatically assume that every interpreter of the same words will arrive at the same meaning. We are limited to our intuitions and probabilities, which are often unconfirmable and rarely exhaust all possible interpretations.

A distinction between interpretation and explanation is in any case not absolute. Our interpretations cannot dispense with objective confirmation, while science cannot ignore the subjective dimension of its language. Theory, like belief, is always an interpretation. Medicine aims to be scientific, but in practice it must rely on the physician's interpretive and speculative as well as deductive skills. A certain school of psychotherapy claims that it does no interpreting because all interpretation is the interpreter's fantasy, but this claim is itself an interpretation.

Meaning coalesces our subjective and objective worlds. By linking our inner and outer perspectives, it encompasses the entire range of conscious experience. We use symbols as perceptible signs of things that are not immediately or fully apprehended. But symbols are more than mere signifiers; they increase our understanding or appreciation of phenomena that would otherwise remain obscure. They not only enable us to relate the unknown to the known, and what is less understood to what is better understood; they also have the special virtue of communicating the complex in concise form when necessary. This is often the case in mathematics.

In the final paragraph of *The Republic*, Plato wrote that the psyche is capable of enduring everything good and everything evil. This capability rests on meaning, which enriches and completes experience beyond what would otherwise be possible. Through memory, history, science, and literature, meaning assuages the adversities of existence. Religion has always relied on symbols to turn the bewildering human adventure into a cosmic drama of hope. Aesthetic and communicative meaning reach an ideal fusion in poetry. Who can show us what it means to be human better than Shakespeare and Homer?

VALUE

Meaning is often taken as equivalent to *value*, because all meaning includes a dimension of feeling, and feeling is the ultimate source of value. As direct reflections of our nature, our values are what they are because of the feelings they arouse in us. Value is necessarily subjective, for it is the *felt quality* of any experience that makes the experience matter. Words such as *pleasure* and *pain*, *good* and *bad*, *beautiful* and *ugly*, gain their significance from feelings. Every value ultimately reflects our organic nature, because all life involves intention or desire, even when it renounces desire. Our values would be neither possible nor intelligible without the physical needs that underlie those values and their fulfillment.

It is clear that our pleasures and pains are part of us, but when we describe things as good or beautiful, we convert our feelings into properties of the external object. The value of such things is not an intrinsic property, however, but a projected judgment. Our qualitative vocabularies gain their meaning from our subjective reactions.

Since the value of anything reflects its harmony or disharmony with our nature, it is beyond logical proof or disproof. A value cannot be true or false as a proposition can be true or false. Inferences and predictions based on value may prove false, but not the value as such. When a woman misjudges a man's character because of his personal charm and marries him, to her eventual regret, his charm was a false basis for prediction; it had its value, but only as charm.

People who cannot feel secure without absolutes attribute their values to a higher source, but there is little doubt that the values of all mortal creatures, from the tiger to the saint, have a natural basis. Since values vary with the nature and predicament of the individual, they can never be equivalent or identical in every situation for every being. The fly evades the swatter only to be swallowed by the bird. It is inherent in our world that what is good for the bird is bad for the fly, just as one person's good may be another person's evil. The irreconcilable needs of different creatures make it impossible for any power, natural or supernatural, to ensure a state of harmony for them all. Like universal justice, universal harmony is an appealing but unrealistic dream.

Values cannot, and need not, be justified by anything ulterior. We enjoy a string quartet because of how the music sounds to us, not because someone called Mozart wrote it. When Santayana wrote "Music is essentially useless, as life is," he was reminding us that value in itself is an end rather than a means and requires no further explanation. The story goes that Beethoven had just finished playing a sonata when a listener asked him to explain it. The composer responded by returning to the piano and playing it again.

The conscious experience of value is what makes life worth living. Without such experience, we would be pieces of machinery, not creatures capable of suffering or joy. When a person inquires into the meaning of life, he is not so much philosophizing as asking, "What has made my life worth living so far, and what value can I find in the time that remains?" Honest answers sometimes offer consolation and sometimes invite depression. Moments of retrospection typically evoke feelings that differ from those previously experienced. But without value—whether felt, remembered, or anticipated—life would have no meaning.

KNOWLEDGE AND TRUTH

Complete objectivity is an illusion, because one cannot eliminate the subjective dimension of experience. Michael Polanyi emphasized this basic insight in his book *Personal Knowledge*. The object-relations psychoanalysts overlook Polanyi's observation when they contrast the "internal" objects of our subjective world with our "external" objects, which we supposedly see as they "really" are. Mother as we *experience* her is an internal object, while mother as she *exists* is an external object. Yet even the "objective" mother exists for us only as our *image* of her reality. As perceived, all objects, internal or external, are still internal in the sense that they are evident to us only through our perceptions. My image of any object is based on my sensory contact with the world. The image is not the object itself but a clue to its presence. Our subjective data can *identify* but cannot actually *be* the objective entities whose reality we instinctively assume.

By pointing beyond itself, the act of knowing offers only a tentative schema or image of our physical world, nothing more. We can know neither physical realities nor another person's inner life except through an act of surmise or interpretation, because we can apprehend with immediate certainty only our own field of consciousness. Knowledge is not disqualified, however, by being a function of the knower as well as a function of the known. There is no point in regretting this limitation, for there is no other way of knowing reality.

Conscious awareness becomes knowledge when it enables us to encounter the world intelligently. Since all knowledge is a provisional record of such encounters, it cannot help being incomplete and is as apt to be false as true. Absolute truth, the complete description of reality, is beyond us; yet if our conception of the world did not conform in part to that reality, the notion of truth would be of little value. The uniqueness of truth is implied in our judgments of probability and our reliance on the data that confirm our hypotheses. One cannot repair a broken machine until a correct diagnosis of the problem supplies a relevant element of truth. Ultimate truth is another matter. It may be compared to the mathematical limit that an infinite series approaches but can never reach. To accept a variety of incompatible "truths," as some thinkers seem willing to do, is an incoherent intellectual position. Proponents of such presumed truths fail to distinguish their different versions of reality, which can only be approximate, from the actual truth at which those approximations aim. All claims of truth would be arbitrary if they could not be tested against a reality that exists in its own right.

REALITY

We speak of reality as if we knew what we were talking about, but whatever it may be, the essence of reality is beyond our grasp. Even the most radical of skeptics cannot free themselves of the conviction that something, whether we comprehend it or not, is there to be reckoned with. Whatever reality may be, it is something we cannot wish out of existence by any effort of will or by any resort to verbal magic. The *real* is as paradoxical as it is impenetrable, for it remains at the same time an ultimate mystery and an ultimate court of appeal. While physicists delve with admirable patience into the fundamental forces and particles that compose the universe, the intrinsic nature and origin of these primal entities remain—and must remain—inaccessible. To complicate things further, reality is not monolithic; there is more than one kind of reality, and reflective observation distinguishes at least three different kinds.

First is the *immediately apparent*, whatever is directly present to awareness. Second is the *world of matter and energy*, the space-time universe in which we temporarily exist. It comprises the natural world and all physical events, including those that generate a third reality. This is *consciousness* itself, the awareness that living things have of the world and of themselves. Consciousness makes the first two forms of reality manifest to a potential observer. We earlier called this faculty our window on the world and noted that, although it must be produced by neurons in the brain, observing the brain never discloses consciousness as such. It enables us to picture space yet cannot be found within space. One cannot experience *consciousness* as such, but only consciousness *of something*, whether thoughts, feelings, or the physical world. In allowing us to contemplate not only what *is* but what *is not*, consciousness grants us a life in both the world of physical reality and the world of imagination.

SPIRIT

Although the word *spirit* often refers to a supernatural essence or entity, here it refers to a unifying function of the personality that gives direction to one's life. The essential aim of spirit is the fulfillment proper to one's nature. Under the guidance of spirit, each of us endeavors to live in a way that conforms to our chosen values, whether as actor or observer.

As an abode of spirit, every conscious being is the center of its universe. One's experience offers a host of possible meanings that vary greatly in what they contribute to one's life. Spirit evaluates all these experiences on a scale ranging from the positive to the negative, from the most enchanting to the most abhorrent. Living becomes *spir-*

itual when one consciously discriminates between such values, unifying consciousness and meaning in the pursuit of one's ideals.

Spirit is a unique development of our physical being. It is a result and not the cause of the brain activity that generates it, and it gains no added significance if it is attributed to a supernatural source.

THE SACRED

Western religion traditionally distinguishes two dimensions of living: the sacred and the secular. The sacred domain is viewed as a superior level of reality, marked by unearthly power and supreme value. Secular existence by contrast is viewed as inferior and earthbound. Each domain occupies its own symbolic region, one above and the other below. Some religions assume there are still lower netherworlds: a Hades or Sheol as abodes of the dead, or a Gehenna or Hell to punish the wicked.

Belief in such domains must have begun before the dawn of history, and it continues in one form or another to the present. In *The Idea of the Holy*, Rudolf Otto affirms that religious experience is a necessary response to what he calls the *numinous*, his term for the supernatural as immediately experienced. For him, the subjective sense of a supernatural presence is as reliable a proof of its objective reality as the odor of a rose proves the presence of the flower. The numinous is a preternatural force that excites wonder, awe, fascination, and at times, terror. It is a *mysterium tremendum*, which invades awareness either as a supernatural process or as a personified Being that may appear as a divine Father, Mother, or Child. Common as such personifications have been in the past, and as much as they are still honored in certain quarters, they possess literal reality only in the eyes of the believer. To a skeptic they are but persuasive symbols. Otto overlooks the presence in the everyday world of everything he discerns in the numinous. The ordinary world is no less amazing, no less mysterious and demonic. Experience of the numinous, whatever its source, always reflects the expectations of the observer. The numinous is never an objective datum; it is *awe objectified*, just as the quality of goodness is *approval objectified*.

In *The Sacred and the Profane*, Mircea Eliade similarly asserts that the sacred differs uniquely from the profane. Like Otto, he holds that the sacred is an objective reality that orients religious consciousness properly to the world. He too has failed to see that every orienting perspective is a subjective interpretation that depends on the observer's assumptions more than on objective data. He deplores the decline of the sacred in today's world and sees nonreligious man as lost in a new "fall" without the absolutes that would enable him to live "in the universal."

More useful is Eliade's insight that life is religious insofar as it is lived by "the whole man." Any religion worthy of the name helps us devote our entire being to our highest goals. If not for its aesthetic and religious dimensions, life might seem entirely profane. Yet the sacred and profane are ultimately inseparable. The sacred and the profane form a single spectrum, its degrees of significance determined by what they mean to the spirit. The awe that life can evoke is limited only by the sensitivity and perceptiveness of the observer.

FREEDOM AND CAUSALITY

Do we enjoy free will or is behavior determined? This question presents us with a pseudodilemma, for once correctly understood, the apparent incompatibility disappears. Freedom does not exclude determinism because freedom is self-determination, the ability of an organism to choose its goals in accord with its own nature. To the extent that it does so, every being contributes to its own fate, for its behavior is never determined solely by external forces or solely by antecedent events. Determinism is nonetheless universal, because we have no choice about the nature of reality or the nature we were born with.

In a rigorous analysis of causation, Mario Bunge, a physicist and philosopher of science, defines freedom as "the *lawful self-determination* of existents on whatever level of reality" (italics in original). In exercising our capacity to choose on the basis of foresight and desire, we are both free and determined. We have a certain degree of freedom even when at odds with ourselves or opposed by forces beyond our control. If I succumb to an irresistible impulse, I reveal not that I lack freedom, but that I have chosen to indulge one impulse at the expense of others. If I submit to a superior force, that decision still marks my freedom to submit or resist. Yet freedom is not unlimited, for we can never contravene the structure of our external or internal reality. To think we could flout these existential constraints at our pleasure would reduce the concept of freedom to absurdity.

We need to understand the world in terms of cause and effect. We do so in accordance with Spinoza's dictum that how external bodies affect a human body must involve at the same time the nature of the human body and the nature of the external body (*Ethics* 2, proposition 16). A freedom not predicated on causality would be of little use to us, because without causality nothing would be predictable. This holds true whether causality is an intrinsic property of the natural world or an illusion created by the human mind. With all our limitations, we still understand the world well enough to survive in it for a certain length of time. Life of every kind survives by counting on the predictability of nature, and such predictability is what the concept of causality signifies. No matter how imperfect our powers of prediction, if we could not rely on certain familiar probabilities, we would have no rational way to carry out our intentions. Nothing brings home the relevance of cause and effect more convincingly than the results of our errors.

FREEDOM AND EVIL

In hoping to reconcile divine omnipotence with human responsibility, religious apologists argue that since God endowed us with free will, the choice of good or evil is up to us. But how qualified are we to make that choice? How clear is the distinction between good and evil? And how free to choose is God himself? Here again, theological casuistry hopes to safeguard the reputation of the Creator by exempting him from responsibility for the flaws of his creation, flaws that no perceptive observer can overlook indefinitely. *Neither error nor evil can be avoided in a world of imperfect creatures, competing needs, and finite resources.* An omniscient and omnipotent Deity must have realized he was creating a world in which there would be no escape from suffering and evil. If he could have done better but chose not to, he himself is implicated in the limitations for which humans are constantly condemned. If he could not have done otherwise, he himself was limited, therefore neither omniscient nor omnipotent. Albert Einstein recognized this contradiction when he wrote:

> I see only with deep regret that God punishes so many of His children for their numerous stupidities, for which only He Himself can be held responsible; in my opinion, only His nonexistence could excuse Him.
>
> Albert Einstein, letter to Edgar Meyer, 1915

Another theological effort to absolve God of his responsibility makes the ironic claim that he created an imperfect world in order to let us enjoy bringing it to perfection—as if fallible mankind could create a better world than one created by an omnipotent and omniscient God.

Life unites freedom and necessity in an inseparable bond. Rational freedom entails both causality and the power of choice, because causality is what makes things predictable, and preference is what makes them matter.

Just as we understand the inanimate world in terms of physical cause and effect, we attribute the behavior of animate beings to their motives. To judge a person's behavior, we need to know what was the intent and how it was achieved. If we fully understood the life experience of criminals and terrorists, we could better understand their actions, for all behavior must have an intelligible basis. Their misconduct is in most cases a response to emotional injury of some kind, whether remembered, anticipated, or misunderstood. Every being pursues what *in its own view* is a prospective good, regardless of subsequent punishment or regret.

There is of course no assurance that our choices will measure up to the wisdom of hindsight. We can no more escape making moral errors than we can escape the natural evils of illness and death. Pious souls must enjoy heartfelt relief that they can reduce the hazards of choice by obeying the will of God. Fanatics no doubt have similar feelings of confidence about following goals they consider beyond dispute.

Evil is not some intrinsically demonic power; it is a name for whatever causes suffering. Some theologians subscribe to Saint Augustine's opinion that evil is simply a lack or insufficiency of good, as if that made the suffering any the less real. This is casuistry that sacrifices the pain of life on the altar of theology. It is essential to realize that evil and good form an inevitable and inseparable pair. Since good and evil are not absolutes but always relative to particular interests, no state of the world can be equally good for every creature.

RESPONSIBILITY

People judge us from the day we are born. In time, they teach us not only who we are but how we should judge ourselves. Those whom we fear or respect are privileged to call us to account for how we behave and even for what we think; to be responsible means having to answer to an authority. Responsibility is not easily accepted, however, because it carries the risk of unfavorable judgment or even punishment. But as we mature, submission to external authority becomes less relevant; we then decide for ourselves what we should do, and we accept responsibility for our decisions.

Taking responsibility is difficult if we are unwilling to risk the outcome. Differing aims can be hard to reconcile. External forces and innate drives both contribute to our behavior, but it is impossible to know which predominate on any given occasion. That uncertainty, however, cannot save us from the consequences of our decisions. Torn between which aims to satisfy and which to resist, we have no choice but to struggle with our internal disunity. When a "should" and a "should not" seem equally essential, we suffer tension or even anxiety until we come to terms with the internal judge who holds us responsible not only for what we have already done but for what we still intend to do.

By rights, an impartial judge ought to hold us responsible only so far as we are free to decide our course of action. Expecting us to answer for behavior we were not free to choose or reject would be neither logical nor fair. But since our actions are neither completely free nor completely determined, how can one know where our responsibility begins and ends? This question constantly plagues a legal system committed to the ideal of justice in assigning guilt and punishment.

In the last analysis, responsibility transcends questions of freedom, justice, and logic. Responsibility implies meeting the demands of life whether we consider them just or unjust, reasonable or unreasonable. Blaming ignorance or the unconscious will not do, even though some behavior may be too painful to admit or recall. Even if a lack of courage leads us to deny responsibility for our behavior, we still will be held accountable in one way or another. Either those concerned will take some action, or our psyches will develop symptoms to remind us of what we were afraid to face.

SELF-KNOWLEDGE AND SELF-ACCEPTANCE

The psyche seems to know most or even all of the truth about itself in the latent self-knowledge that Harry Stack Sullivan called "prehension." The self, on the other hand, in its commitment to maintaining pride, is always susceptible to self-deception. This discrepancy accounts for symptoms that escape our conscious understanding. Errors we cannot hide invite humiliation, and those we cannot acknowledge entail anxiety. Yet despising ourselves for our mistakes is a further error, for our mistakes are what can teach us the most. Self-acceptance is essential, for in some way everything that exists has its intrinsic worth. But self-acceptance differs from self-centeredness. Healthy self-esteem requires seeing ourselves just as we are. There is no need to deny what we are or renounce our natural self-interest, so long as we take responsibility for both.

In his *Guide of the Perplexed*, the Jewish philosopher Moses Maimonides wrote, "The Universe does not exist for man's sake, but each being exists for its own sake, and not because of some other thing." Santayana made a related point when he wrote, "A free mind does not measure the worth of anything by the worth of anything else" ("Cloud Castles" in *Soliloquies in England*). This insight is easily overshadowed by self-doubt and the fear of being misjudged. While we cannot be fully human *without* others, we find it difficult to be completely ourselves in living *with* them. Even if utopian harmony were desirable, it is an impossible goal. Created to be human beings, not ants or bees, we must make the best of a problematic existence in which we can neither totally flout nor totally fulfill all that life requires. A Zen master reminds us:

> A blind man, even while blind, is fundamentally whole and perfect. The same is true of a deaf man. If a deaf mute suddenly regained his hearing, his perfection would no longer be that of a deaf mute. Were this saucer on the table to be broken, each segment would be wholeness itself. Things are neither perfect nor imperfect; they are what they are. Everything has absolute worth, hence nothing can be compared with anything else. A tall man is tall, a short man is short, that is all you can say.
>
> *The Three Pillars of Zen*, ed. Philip Kapleau

MORALITY

Every community imposes moral obligations on its members, and those obligations inevitably conflict at times with individual self-will.

The obligatory nature of such rules has led theologians to consider them supernaturally ordained. Since this pits human will against divine will, only divine grace can save mankind from the sin of disobedience. Such morality makes the error of assuming, *per impossibile,* universal agreement about values held to be absolute or divine. Commitment to an immutable system fosters indifference to the varied needs of those whom the system is intended to serve.

A naturalistic analysis explains moral behavior differently. As a human expression of mutual concern and the ability to transcend self-will when necessary, morality can be better understood as a communal effort to reconcile self-interest with social interest. Since these interests, like the interests of marriage partners, frequently waver between being complementary and competitive, their predictable failure to coincide in all cases must occasion moral dilemmas. Such conflicts are unavoidable.

Behavior that is truly moral rests on empathy. This term does not mean *having* the same feelings as another person, but *understanding* those feelings with enough concern to act in that person's interest. Moral behavior is often blocked by conflicting priorities that disregard human needs. People are always at liberty to defy moral standards if they expect to gain more by their defiance than they would lose by being caught and punished. Many people pay little but lip service to moral rules unless influenced by fear of punishment or hope of reward. Such people are morally juvenile, and what they practice is pseudo-morality. Feeling a genuine concern for others is a much better basis for morality than the instilling of guilt.

Empathy forms the basis of the silver rule of Hillel, a Talmudic sage of the first century. A pagan once ordered him, "Summarize the Torah for me while I stand on one foot." Without hesitation, Hillel replied, "What is hateful to you, do not do to your fellow. That is the whole Torah. The rest is commentary. Go and study." (*Babylonian Talmud, Sabbat* 31a). Hillel's logic can be stated explicitly:

(1) If you and your fellow have similar feelings, then

(2) what is hateful to you will be hateful to him, and

(3) if his feelings matter to you, then

(4) you will not do to him what is hateful to you.

This reasoning is valid only if your fellow's feelings actually matter to you, for it rests on an assumption there is no way to enforce. Even more concisely, the golden rule as stated in *Leviticus* 19:18 commands: "You shall love your neighbor as yourself," another imperative easier to proclaim than to obey or enforce.

If we ask why anyone should obey this commandment, the devout will answer, "Because God commanded it through his prophet, Moses." The point, however, is not whether God commanded it, but what *justified* the commandment. If morality is not justified by its human consequences, adducing an ulterior authority becomes irrelevant. As a cosmic power, God personifies the force of natural law, but as a source of morality, God represents the indispensable role of social standards in human life. Albert Einstein understood this when he wrote, "Morality is of the highest importance—but for us, not for God."

The notion dies hard that without supernatural sanctions there would be no morality. In Dostoevsky's novel *The Brothers Karamazov*, Ivan asserts that if not for God, everything would be permitted. This is true if *God* represents genuine human empathy, but false if it means that except for divine sanctions there would be no moral behavior. People who can identify with others require no supernatural sanctions, while people who hate are undeterred by sanctions of any kind, human or divine. In any case, whatever happens has in fact already been permitted—God, law, and morality notwithstanding.

Morality owes its force to social necessity, its weakness to human inconsistency. There is no easy way to resolve the tension between the requirements of social existence and one's innate desire for personal liberty. When values are incompatible, moral conflicts resist rational solution. The difficulty of resolving moral disagreements by reason alone dismays the moralist, whose principles, no matter how well intended, cannot successfully abolish the conflicting forces of self-interest. Any morality held to be unchallengeable will sooner or later prove to be immoral, for it can never accommodate all eventualities and often ends in self-contradiction. Consider for example the death penalty, which permits authorities to punish a murderer by committing the very same crime. Such pseudomorality has justified many socially sanctioned crimes *ad majorem Dei gloriam* (for the greater glory of God). Whoever attempts to separate the good from the bad will find how difficult it can often be to tell them apart.

DUALISM

Although we tend to think in polar opposites (black and white, good and evil), most phenomena are not binary. While it is convenient to name the extreme ends of a continuum, almost everything in life occurs not at the extremes but somewhere in between. Even this is a simplification, because most characteristics that we conceive as opposites are not mutually exclusive. One can feel love and hate for the same person. It is impossible to be entirely good or entirely evil, because within every human being lies something of the sinner and something of the saint. No one is completely innocent or completely guilty, a point Jesus made when he told those prepared to stone an adulteress, "He that is without sin among you, let him first cast a stone at her" (John 8:7). Even life and death are not mutually exclusive, for in every living body, old cells die off and are replaced by new ones. In a larger perspective, the birth and death of individual creatures allows a species to renew itself continually. Without death, we would not have life.

The Chinese concept of Yin and Yang includes the understanding that each quality contains the potentiality for its opposite, and that in time, one becomes the other. This scheme takes the ends of the continuum and joins them to form a circle. Keep sailing to the east and you will end up in the west. Morning light contains latent darkness which increases through the afternoon until day turns to night. Peace always contains conflict that can escalate into war; in war there is always the possibility of making peace. In this way, empires rise and fall, allies become enemies, and enemies become friends. The harder one tries to live a faultless life, the more one is overpowered by the flaws that lie dormant in every human being.

CHANGE

Our conceptions of the world are inevitably shaped by our nature and our needs, which produce even our dreams. Could the worlds envisioned in our dreams be superior to this one? The philosopher Leibniz held that no other world could be significantly better, because conflict and evil are intrinsic features of the universe. Voltaire then caricatured Leibniz in *Candide* as the absurdly optimistic Doctor Pangloss, who pronounced this the best of all possible worlds.

The fact is that almost every living creature, from man to microbe, depends for survival on eating or destroying other living things. The true Lord of the universe is Change, and its inevitable consequence is mortality. Without change there could be no conscious experience, no pleasure or pain, no life or death; nor could any conceivable power even have generated our paradoxical reality. The human dream of immortality ignores the transitory nature of all that exists.

The universe continues on its massively indifferent course, leaving us to find our way as best we can. So far as we know, life can be lived and fulfilled only in the transitory present, not in some imaginary celestial realm. The culmination of any cosmic design is unlikely to fall within our mortal scope. If a cosmic intelligence is at work, it bears little similarity to our own, for its astonishing fertility is matched only by its detachment from the joys and sufferings of the beings it created and imbued with unfulfillable longings. Unless we have the wisdom and imagination to make the most of reality as it is, all we can do is follow our fascinating and troubled course to the end.

ON REASON
AND RELIGION

There are questions for which we have no answers, questions on which universal agreement has never been reached and probably never will be. The human mind nevertheless refuses to give up asking them. Where did the universe come from and where does life come from? Is there a personal God who is concerned with our fate? What is our purpose in living? Why must we die, and what happens after death? Why are we subject to natural disasters, accidents, sickness, and man's inhumanity to man? Why does tragedy strike some of us and leave others untouched? What makes a good life? If we do our best to live as we should, why are we made to suffer?

Religion has been humanity's most ancient and determined attempt to find such answers. In the course of history, a great many religions have undertaken to allay the uncertainty of human life. At its best, religion enhances life; at its worst, it makes life more contentious. Yet a need for religion in some form is unmistakable in the intensity with which the devout embrace it, the skeptical reject it, and the fanatical carry it to extremes.

The invention of religion was an extraordinary inspiration; it must have given our ancestors profound relief from existential uncertainty. They could now refer the mysteries of existence to personified forces that exerted power while remaining invisible. When old gods became outmoded, they were replaced by newer gods who reflected humanity's changing needs. Reliance on supernatural direction continues for many to the present day.

The diversity of religious beliefs offers fertile grounds for contention. Universal agreement about the ultimate questions is neither possible nor necessary. Some minds need to understand things literally, while others are naturally predisposed to symbolic thinking. We are far from resolving the confusion that arises from the inability to distinguish between the symbol and what it symbolizes. Confusing faith with fact perpetuates the incoherence of civilization. At best, religion helps people confront the mysteries of life without ignoring reason. A civilized intelligence acknowledges its inherent limitations and respects the right of others to come to their own conclusions.

Faith and *belief* are often treated as practically synonymous, but they need to be distinguished. By *faith*, I do not mean a religious tradition or an intellectual conviction, but an instinctive confidence that the world and our nature are in fundamental accord, that we belong in the universe, and that our existence has value. *Faith* is something intrinsic and primary. Preverbal and untaught, it requires no logical demonstration or objective proof. In a world of uncertainty, no one can live without faith of some kind. It affirms our right, as Spinoza put it, to persist in our own being.

But insecure as humans are, even the innate gift of faith needs added support. All human cultures therefore fortify their faith with beliefs, rituals, and myths that promote a sense of security in this formidable universe. *Belief* is a secondary acquisition, gained through language and indoctrination. Beliefs are therefore particular to a specific culture and individual, whereas faith is a more universal human endowment. Religious beliefs may include philosophical assumptions, dogmas, and more or less plausible stories. Much religious controversy depends on whether these beliefs are taken as unassailable fact or metaphorical guides.

The greater the uncertainties of existence, the more readily people are drawn to compensatory beliefs whose validity may be just as uncertain. Even though such beliefs can be persuasive and reassuring, they rest on premises that are no sooner put into words than they ensnare us in paradox and improbability. People of course differ considerably about why they accept some beliefs and reject others. For skeptics, logic and evidence come first. For others, the literal sense matters less than the illuminating metaphors and symbols that convey the deeper meaning. If religious conviction goes so far as denying others the right to think for themselves, it runs counter to the basic religious aim of peaceful coexistence. Adherence to the literal truth of religious beliefs is not essential to religious experience.

Many people claim to possess the truth, but there is much in religion for which *truth* is not the correct label. The concept of truth is properly applicable only in the realms of logical reasoning and natural process. Applying it elsewhere is an error, for truth implies fidelity not to hope or desire but to unquestionable or confirmable data. To call a religion true erects an edifice of belief on a foundation of emotional need. Insofar as religion is a spiritual search or devotion to an ideal, it cannot be true or false as a statement of fact can be true or false. Even divine fiat cannot convert a subjective aspiration into the objective truth that many religions claim to possess.

The dilemma posed by the irreconcilability of religious belief with reason is captured in the famous paradoxical statement written by the Church Father Tertullian in the second century: *Credo quia impossibile est* (I believe because it is impossible, *De Carne Christi*, 5). This confession that Christian dogma transcends reason, or that faith defies logic, was an early recognition that a purely logical view of the world is incomplete. In medieval times, Dante appreciated the same tension between belief and reason when he wrote in *Purgatorio* (Canto 3.37) that those who hope to penetrate the mystery of the Trinity are mad; they should be content with the *quia* (the *because*).

This dilemma can be resolved. Dogmatic affirmation of a particular religious belief can conflict with reason or objective data, but faith as an inborn conviction of one's place and value in the world is something altogether different. Faith of this kind cannot be in conflict with reason or facts. Believers often confuse the question of a dogma's validity with the essential aim of religion. That aim, coming to terms with our existence in a universe that confounds human reason and desire, is independent of any religious dogma. Faith is not a claim to special knowledge but the investment of our total being in the experience of living.

Religious fundamentalists, rather than admitting their fear of uncertainty, try to suppress it by claiming to know what is unknowable. They find reassurance in adhering to a strictly literal understanding of their sacred texts. They claim their understanding is not an interpretation but the word of God himself, therefore the one and only true meaning. But any reading is an interpretation, whether one sees it as literal or not. It is impossible to substantiate a claim that words on a page came directly from God. Reasonable readers accept that human beings, perhaps divinely inspired but human nonetheless, wrote the words that came to be included in the Bible. How is one to know if a writer had only one meaning in mind? Who can know with certainty the intent of a writer who lived in distant times, was the product of another culture, and used a different language? Jesus spoke in Aramaic; his words were remembered and recorded, long after his death, in Greek; we now read an English translation. At each stage along the way, there is interpretation. Why then should we deprive ourselves of further interpretations?

Fundamentalists claim to know what God thinks. But in a compilation like the Bible, one finds a variety of views. If all those views are true, what does one do about the contradictions? The choice of which texts fundamentalists defend and which they ignore can be revealing about their underlying motivations. They generally aim to preserve a belief system or way of life in which they feel invested. There was a time when people defended slavery by pointing out its presence in the Bible. As the Episcopal Bishop John Shelby Spong points out, zealots who use biblical quotations to justify intolerance or hate are overlooking an important question:

It did not occur to those quoting this Scripture to raise questions about what kind of God was assumed in this verse, or whether or not they could worship such a God. Since they could not identify themselves with those who were the victims of this cruelty, the God to whom they ascribed this victimizing power did not appear to them to be seriously compromised.

John Shelby Spong, *Rescuing the Bible from Fundamentalism*

To impute prejudice to God and to ignore the parts of the Bible that reject such prejudice are hallmarks of religious extremism. Spong believes the only concern of a person who uses biblical texts in this way is "to maintain that person's prejudice, to enable that person to avoid having to change destructive attitudes." Unfortunately, fundamentalist traditions in all the major religions have been guilty, at one time or another, of using religious rhetoric to lend God's name to their political agendas.

The exaggerated vehemence with which a person insists on his position indicates the defensive nature of his argument. Feeling that any criticism of his religious views amounts to an attack on him personally, he redoubles his efforts to convince others he possesses the truth in order to avoid confronting the contradictions or uncertainties he is unable to face.

Expecting religion to solve the riddles of existence without the help of reason ensures that religion will embody the paradoxes it is supposed to dispel. A tradition that counters the insecurity of existence with dogmatic contradictions only guarantees further insecurity. The faculty of reason also has its limitations, but if we fail to use our full potential as we wrestle with the eternal questions, we lose the wholeness for which we turn to religion in the first place.

Reason cannot deny the essence of religion, which is not so much a knowing as a caring. It is an effort less to explain the world than to make life worth living in a world that is unexplainable. Whether religious conviction is factually valid or invalid counts for little in comparison to the support it offers a soul adrift in the cosmos, or the message that man should be concerned about his fellow man. The ethical teachings in religion are not justified by alleging a supernatural or miraculous source. Ethical principles are validated only when their application contributes to a more harmonious coexistence.

There is much in religious experience that is independent of reason or belief. Religious observance gives one the assurance of belonging to a history and a tradition. Absorption in a meaningful ritual yields a sense of fulfillment that cannot be attained by words alone. The power of ritual outweighs any need for further justification, and can be experienced by believers and nonbelievers alike. Through ritual, worshipers express their pursuit of the good, their rejection of evil, and their acceptance of a world beyond their comprehension or control. In the mystical traditions, Hasidic Jews and Sufi Muslims express their devotion in ecstatic song and dance. Their religious life would be incomplete without such total involvement of body and soul. The great existential questions do not trouble us during these moments of inner and outer accord.

Belief in a Supreme Being must nevertheless arise from a profound human need. Theists feel certain that an unseen deity created the universe and guarantees its ultimate meaning, even though all attempts to prove the existence of such a Being simply beg the question. Theology has been flattered as queen of the sciences, but her queenship presides over a world of inconclusive speculation. If belief in God springs from subrational depths, the lack of confirmation becomes immaterial. Whatever doubts skeptics harbor about the existence of a supernatural deity, they cannot deny the reassurance that theists derive from such belief.

Belief in an afterlife, like belief in God, persists as an expression of hope despite the absence of evidence or proof. The call by Jesus to renounce the world of suffering and await the Kingdom of God proved premature, but many people still expect to be compensated in an afterlife for what they have missed or suffered on earth. This hope overlooks the uncertainty that dogs all eschatological prognosis. Whoever hopes to meet the Messiah face to face may have to outlast the present world. Franz Kafka put an unerring finger on the issue when he wrote,

"Only our concept of time makes it possible to speak of the Day of Judgment by that name; in reality it is a summary court in perpetual session" (*Reflections on Sin, Pain, Hope, and the True Way*).

How does one determine the nature of a divine reality? This question has never been answered to everyone's satisfaction. The biblical prohibition of idolatry can be taken as a warning that it is impossible to capture the essence of an ineffable God. As soon as one describes God in human terms, as believers inevitably do, the concept of God is belittled by its reduction to a human level. All one can say is that the idea of God represents a reality that transcends our comprehension.

If reliance on a benevolent Creator allows believers to reject as absurd an impersonal world of natural law, it also allows them to overlook a still greater absurdity: a benevolent Creator who countenances the suffering of the beings to whom he gave life and feelings. Even the greatest of medieval poets seems to have sacrificed logical consistency to his theological system when he ignores the torments of the damned by ending the *Paradiso* with the oft-quoted line:

> *l'amor che move il sole e l'altre stelle*
> the love that moves the sun and the other stars.
> Dante, *Paradiso* (Canto 33.145)

Would "love" move the stars but condemn the sinner to eternal punishment? Referring to the Deity as love characterizes him as a human ideal. But if the universe finally proves indifferent to our ideals, are we to abandon them? Confronted with dilemmas that baffle the conscious mind, the psyche summons from its depths answers that a bewildered seeker embraces with relief. Such evocations are in essence reassuring dreams that sustain our hopes and ideals.

The philosopher George Santayana offers a proposal to simplify the perpetual debate about the existence of God. This statement is found in *The Realm of Spirit*, the last volume of his final series, *The Realms of Being*.

> When people ask, Does God exist? the question is really verbal.
> They are asking whether the reality signified by the notion of God,
> if we understood that reality better, could still bear the name of God,
> or had better be designated by some other word. This is at bottom
> the whole question in dispute between theists and atheists.

Santayana preferred to say nothing about what position people might
take if they knew for certain whether the God-reality is personal or
impersonal.

There are theists who maintain that if we deny a personal God, life
is not only an insoluble riddle but a tragedy. Without faith in the divine,
they see the human predicament as a hopeless paradox, and history as
a tale without meaning. Yet God or no God, the world is still beyond
our comprehension. If there is some kind of deity, his existence is a
cosmic mockery. Born as we are into a universe of impenetrable mystery, our tragedy is not in denying a God whose reality is unconfirmable, but in failing to earn such fulfillment as is possible for finite
beings in a world of uncertainty. Whether it be our lot to laugh or to cry,
to suffer or to enjoy, our salvation can only be of our own making.

When there is reason to doubt the factual truth of a biblical text,
such as the story in Genesis that God created the world in six days, it
puts fundamentalists in a quandary. They cannot accept having doubt
cast on teachings that grant them a positive vision of the universe.
Unhappy with the sterility of the scientific world view, they take refuge
in a literal reading of the biblical story, which they find both more com-
prehensible and more comforting. In an effort to make their approach
more palatable to departments of education, creationists have recently
taken to the term "intelligent design," which enables them to evade
frankly referring to God. But the alleged intelligence observed in our
perplexing world leaves a good deal to be desired. (On this point, one
should read the article "Accidental Elegance" by Mary Beth Saffo.)

Creationists emphasize the improbability that living matter, say a
protein molecule, could have arisen at random, by the laws of chance.
Yet the very use of the concept of chance confesses our human limita-

tions. The universe is anything but random, for matter and energy are organized down to the last infinitesimal detail. To assume that a divine Being created or organized the universe is merely to personify nature. Must there be a conscious prime mover simply because we prefer anthropomorphic explanations? Why cannot nature be *causa sui*, her own first cause?

How the universe came into existence eludes our comprehension and is likely to do so indefinitely. The attempt by science to understand the natural world through evidence and reason may well be imperfect, but the fundamentalist's willingness to bypass reason adds nothing to our understanding. Belief in creationism is motivated not by a desire to investigate the universe but by a psychological need for certainty. Clinging to the literal truth of biblical texts advances neither science nor religion.

Correctly understood, reason does not contradict faith and faith does not contradict reason. Many scientists describe themselves as people of faith and feel no conflict between their religion and the scientific pursuit. Science is man's use of observation and reason in an effort to learn how nature operates. Religion is man's attempt to reconcile himself to his place in a world that is beyond human comprehension. The language of science is precise and literal; the language of religion is poetic and symbolic. Neither science nor religion will ever answer all of our questions. An enlightened believer reads the book of Genesis not as history or science but as myth, as poetry that expresses our wonder at the mysterious world we live in. No amount of scientific understanding diminishes that sense of mystery and delight.

Those who are content with the literal sense of their religious texts deprive themselves of the benefit of the deeper implications of what they believe. Many a traditional text has turned out to harbor levels of meaning that are missed by a literal approach. Merely exposing the improbability of the literal story does not negate the value of a religious text. An enlightened reader may reject a literal interpretation and still probe it for other kinds of significance. The Catholic writer Flannery O'Connor once wrote, "For me a dogma is only a gateway to contemplation and is an instrument of freedom and not of restriction" (*The Habit of Being*). Approaching such passages as poetry, myth, or ethical guidance, one can discover metaphoric and symbolic reverberations that deepen one's understanding and appreciation throughout a lifetime. In this spirit Matthew Arnold wrote, "The strongest part of our religion today is its unconscious poetry" ("The Study of Poetry," *Essays in Criticism*).

When symbolic thought is not tolerated, constructive communication is hampered as well. In 1529, Martin Luther and Huldrych Zwingli met with their circle in order to iron out their differences and present a united front to the Catholics. Luther quoted Christ's words from Matthew 26:26, "Hoc est corpus meum" (this is my body), and firmly insisted they must be taken literally. Zwingli immediately pointed out that here the word *est* (Latin for "is") really means *significat* ("represents" or "stands for"). To counteract Luther's literalism, he cited the words of Jesus: "It is the spirit that quickeneth; the flesh profiteth nothing" (John 6:63), from which he concluded that Jesus meant us to eat his body not literally and physically but symbolically and spiritually. As Luther refused to consider any interpretation but his own, he and Zwingli quickly brought the discussion to a close with an angry interchange. When differences about dogma lead to hostility instead of mutual comprehension, even sincerely religious people can forget their principles and lose their way. Recognizing the validity of symbolic thought would go a long way toward dispelling much unnecessary controversy in the field of religion.

The soul will always need symbols and myths in its search for a haven in a perplexing universe, just as it needs to pray for integrity in the face of the our human contradictions. Although faith cannot dispel the demonic reality that envelops us, it can enable us to encounter that reality with our whole being. *This total encounter is the core of religion;* all conscious systems of belief are secondary.

To endure existence requires faith in the value of life, even with its unavoidable uncertainties and suffering. Religious believers dismayed by the inscrutable nature of the world can at least draw support from their trust in an ultimately benevolent Deity. But what sustains the confidence of the agnostics, the skeptics, or the atheists? Given the natural curiosity that animates all human beings, they too search for meaning in a universe of endless mystery. The fulfillment that they derive from that search generates a sense of awe and a feeling of gratitude that can be expressed in either religious or secular terms. The wonders of existence can be savored by anyone able to endure its terrors, although life's ordeals show that the divine is also the demonic. Life, value, and purpose must exist potentially in the ultimate nature of energy—in the essence of the subatomic quark. Why quarrel with calling this extraordinary potentiality divine? When the symbols of theism are properly understood, they are no longer grounds for contention; they are poetic terms for this cosmic potentiality, a tribute one cannot begrudge. Religious vistas are essentially waking dreams. Why disallow another's dream because it is not ours?

THE WORLD
OF RELIGION

Over the millennia of human history, people in different times and cultures have developed a great variety of religious ideas, attitudes, and beliefs. This chapter will briefly survey some of the major religious traditions, making no attempt to describe them exhaustively, merely highlighting salient principles and adding personal observations where they may be of interest.

JUDAISM

In a remote past, Judaism broke with its neighboring religions through a stubborn adherence to monotheism. More than a religion, the complex culture of the Jews has persisted through centuries of misunderstanding and persecution until the present day. Although they did not form a political entity from the year 70 until 1948, the Jews survived through fidelity to their unique religious tradition. Judaism drew much and altered much from other cultures, but its exact origin is lost in a past on which the biblical record throws a largely mythical light. Its historical course having been well documented, however, I can summarize its most enduring elements.

129

The tradition rests on the Hebrew scriptures (the Christian Old Testament) which consist of the five books of Torah (the Pentateuch), the major and minor Prophets, and the Writings, a miscellaneous collection that includes Psalms, Proverbs, the Song of Songs, and Ecclesiastes. Jews refer to these scriptures as a whole by the acronym *Tanakh*, formed by the initial letters of the Hebrew words for Torah, Prophets, and Writings. This collection was canonized during the first century of the Christian era. Torah, which basically means teaching, has grown in time to embrace the gamut of Jewish learning, including the Talmud.

The Talmud is a unique collection of rabbinical rulings and arguments, which Pharisaic rabbis began assembling at some time in the third Christian century. It reached its present form in about the year 600. All Talmudic rulings had to be justified by reference to specific scriptural texts. At first, those rulings were passed down orally, but later they were recorded in written form as the Oral Torah, which the rabbis thereafter treated as equal in authority to the scriptural Torah. The legal rulings form the Halakhah (the Way); the nonlegal narratives and homilies compose the Aggadah (stories, parables). The Talmud has to this day been supplemented by rabbinical commentary adapted to the changing needs of the Jewish world. The biblical text itself, kept scrupulously intact, has also been elucidated in Midrash, a collection of explanatory and interpretive commentary enriched by imaginative expansion of the biblical narratives.

Kabbalah expresses the conviction that Torah harbors esoteric meaning beyond the plain sense of the text. This mystical development was furthered by an influential medieval commentary, the Zohar (The Book of Splendor). Using original symbols to bridge the gulf between the real and the ideal, Kabbalists even proposed that Torah was the blueprint for the universe and that the Hebrew alphabet served God as building blocks for the Creation—an inversion of causality in celebration of Torah and the divinity that pervades the world. Torah and God were accordingly joined to form the unitary wellspring of existence.

Torah is not a philosophy but a divinely prescribed system of living, one that bases earthly fulfillment on heavenly directives. Not all Jews accept this system, for many see the traditional text as a human document open to varying interpretations. Some agree with Spinoza, who saw *God* and *nature* as different names for the same reality. For traditional Judaism, however, human beings are not just works of nature; they are the unique creation of a God who dictates moral principles and instills guilt in the sinner. Such a God is the Lord of a world that cannot escape error and evil without divine help. This fusion or confusion of an ethical order with natural process is typical of the Judaic conception of the divine. The biblical God resists definition, but in the rich variety of his attributes, he mirrors the world he created. If God made man in his own divine image, man proceeded to give God a human image in return.

The Bible allows Yahweh/Elohim (the two most common names of God) to reveal himself in all his complexity. *Elohim* stands for justice and *Yahweh* for mercy, but God has many other names and attributes, the most remarkable being his enigmatic reply to Moses: "Ehyeh Asher Ehyeh" (Exodus 3:14), which could mean "I am who I am" or "I will be as I will be," and was translated by Harold Bloom as "I will be where and when I will be" (*Jesus and Yahweh*). An analytical prism resolves God's supernatural radiance into its natural components, for the scriptural God fuses attributes of nature with attributes of man. As natural process, he creates a universe and dispenses life and death. As moral authority, he commands, punishes, and forgives, always for human reasons. He condescends to talk and debate with patriarchs and prophets, at times even allowing Abraham and Moses to win the argument.

Moses speaks for God in the great directive: "You shall love the Lord your God with all your heart and with all your soul and with all your might" (Deut. 6:5). This command involves more than devotion to the ideal; it implies that God represents the reality of a world we must love if we are to endure it. The relation of Judaism to its God is further cemented in the daily affirmation of the *Sh'ma*, which proclaims that the Lord is not only One but Unique. Its communal recital assures Jews that they are part of a coherent universe. As creator and destroyer, God represents the flux of nature, which generates and annihilates all transitory things. Jews who obey his commands, whether they seem reasonable or not, acknowledge their dependence on an ultimately unfathomable reality.

God's delight in life reflects the determination of all living creatures to survive in the face of adversity. The liturgy carries the praise of God to what seems a naive extreme until it is understood as an affirmation of life in defiance of every insult this world can inflict. To affirm that one loves God therefore concentrates in a single phrase one's gratitude for the gift of life, one's submission to the real, and one's pursuit of the ideal. In its entreaties for the redemption of mankind, the daily prayer book reminds us that our ideals are still unachieved, while confidence in the arrival of the Messiah maintains our trust in their ultimate fulfillment. Isaiah writes, "Behold, I create new heavens and a new earth. . . . They shall not hurt nor destroy in all my holy mountain, saith the Lord" (Isaiah 65:17, 25). He ascribes these words to God, but they voice an unmistakably human longing to reconcile man with nature and to overcome the cruelty and incoherence of existence.

We have already noted God's human character. Justice and mercy, the great polar attributes of God in action, are human ideals that humanity has never been able to reconcile. God can therefore assume either a masculine or feminine role as needed. As a father figure, he is a ruler and a judge. *Rahamim* (mercy) comes from the Hebrew word for womb, representing the maternal aspect of God. The *Shekhinah* (dwelling), again a feminine noun, refers to the divine influence as it dwells on earth.

God forbids his portrayal by any image, yet he behaves as a person, and an inconsistent person at that. He is praised for his benevolence but unhesitatingly decrees stoning for the fallible beings who disobey his laws. God's motivation is especially problematic when he orders Abraham to bind Isaac for sacrifice (Genesis 22). Was Abraham's loyalty to be a model for all mankind? Was it to help pagans recognize the self-sacrificial devotion that monotheistic faith inspires? Or was the divine power who endowed us with our hopes and desires reminding us that in the end we have no choice but to give up everyone and everything we love?

The God of Judaism is a divinity who assigned his people a set of dictates that only qualified rabbis were authorized to interpret. When those rabbis realized that certain archaic rulings in the Torah were no longer reasonable or humane, they did not annul them but ingeniously reinterpreted them while keeping the sacred text intact. The penalty of an eye for an eye, a notoriously misunderstood example, was never exacted literally. Talmudic explication made it possible to apply more acceptable penalties. The rabbis thus devised a system of living open to continuous development. Rabbi Ben Bag Bag said of the Torah, "Turn it and turn it over again, for everything is in it" (Mishnah, Avot 5.25), thus treating the sacred text not as a celestial encyclopedia but as a flexible and enduring guide to a Jewish existence. Rabbinic wisdom of this kind enabled Judaism to survive for two thousand years.

The Jewish approach to Talmudic interpretation is well illustrated in the story of a controversy about the ritual purity of a certain type of oven (Bava Mezia 59a, b). Rabbi Eliezer, a respected authority, pronounced it ritually pure, but all his colleagues thought otherwise. When Eliezer called for divine support of his opinion, God answered with a series of miracles that defied the laws of nature, and a heavenly voice endorsed Eliezer's view. The rabbis rejected God's intervention on the grounds that Halakhic rulings are made on earth, not in heaven, and are legitimized only by logical thinking and rabbinic consensus. When God heard their decision, he laughed, saying "My children have defeated me, my children have defeated me!" It is significant that God did not object to being overruled, but acknowledged the right of the rabbis to fulfill divine purpose in their own way. By that time, Halakhic decisions rested solidly on the judgment of a rabbinic majority, whose human rulings had become exempt from celestial intervention. This story even suggests that the sages were not altogether overawed by God but were subliminally aware that in some sense he was a human creation.

Many ultra-Orthodox Jews still close their eyes to any evidence that Torah is a human creation. Some even assume that it entitles them to reoccupy the entire area of biblical Israel. Fearing that the Judaism they know and love might vanish, the most extreme maintain that Jews who question the literal truth of Torah read themselves out of Judaism altogether. The disagreements that pit fundamentalists against critical thinkers have led to a major breach in the relative solidarity of Judaism as it existed until recent times. Yet that solidarity was never monolithic; from the beginning, the Hebrews were always quarreling with Moses.

Torah and Halakhah, unique to be sure, are no more and no less divinely inspired than any other monument of human genius. Their human origin, visible on every page, reveals them as venerable rather than infallible. The vehemence with which the ultra-Orthodox reject this position shows their understandable anxiety about the fate of Judaism, but it also unwittingly betrays an unacknowledged lack of confidence in their convictions. While Halakhah offers the security and discipline of submission to a sacred authority, as an end in itself it is capable of belying its own ideal. Is it divine wisdom or male anxiety that forbids contemporary Orthodoxy to revise its traditional treatment of women? If a skeptic finds Torah divine, it is only figuratively, as an extraordinary but imperfect effort of the human spirit to transcend its limitations.

What does Judaism offer today? It unites Jews in a communal bond and sanctifies their lives in three ways: through study of Torah, observance of Halakhah, and submission to a divinely ordained moral order. Halakhah prescribes values that are not limited to the Halakhic system, for the core of these values is respect for life and human dignity. Jewish ritual can be appreciated as poetry, not as law, yet even as poetry its observance enriches and disciplines Jewish life.

Political changes in the West have nevertheless made it much easier for Jews to live and think as they please. This freedom has fragmented the tradition. Some Jews have abandoned it, others cling to it with passion, and still others are experimenting with novel alternatives. The Jews of today are accordingly free to avail themselves of ultra-Orthodoxy, modern Orthodoxy, Conservative Judaism, Reform

Judaism, Reconstructionism, or secular skepticism—yet all see themselves as Jews. This range of choice has increased the frequency of intermarriage and creates grave alarm in those who fear the tradition is at risk of disappearing.

Many modern Jews are therefore caught between their need for autonomy and their concern for survival as a coherent group. Less dependent than their ancestors on a religious community, they are less ready to sacrifice personal choice for the sake of their tradition, despite its great antiquity and unique significance. Like all theistic belief, Judaism exists in a state of unresolved tension so long as myth is confused with demonstrable reality. And like every historical religion, it lacks a unified and rational foundation. There has never been only one right way to be a Jew. To think otherwise is to close one's eyes to the history of the tradition. In the face of their many differences, Jews need to ask themselves which should come first: that which divides them or that which unites them?

CHRISTIANITY

Christianity is an offspring of Judaism, but it has outgrown its parent to become the most widespread religion in the world today. Christianity complicates the idea of monotheism by centering its focus around the figure of Jesus Christ, who provides a divine link between man and God. God is personified as a transcendent Being, at once complex and unitary but ultimately undefinable. In standard Catholic theology, God is a divine Trinity, a paradoxical Three-in-One, consisting of a Father who created the universe; a Son, part human and part divine, who redeems the sinner; and a Holy Spirit who sanctifies an imperfect world. This same God has also granted human beings the dangerous freedom to choose sin or salvation at their own discretion. Although sin and evil would seem to be paradoxical elements in a world created by a benevolent God, the evil dimension serves to justify the indispensable role of Christianity as a religion of redemption.

The basic story of Christianity is that Jesus, the son of God, born of a virgin mother, was the long-awaited Messiah whom God chose to offer in mortal incarnation as a sacrifice to redeem humanity from its sins. As Christ, Jesus earned the redemption of humanity through his own suffering and death. His divinity then ensured his miraculous resurrection. For Christians, belief in the divinity of Jesus is both necessary and sufficient for salvation. To reject that belief is to choose perdition.

Almost nothing is known with certainty about the man Jesus. The gospels were written long after his death. We know that Jesus the man lived and died as a Jew. The name Jesus is a Hellenized form of Joshua (which means "Yahweh saves" or "Yahweh will save"), and the term *Christ* is the Greek translation of the title *Messiah*. There were messianic elements in Judaism during the period of Jesus' life, but the term *Messiah* could refer to a hope for deliverance from Roman occupation as well as deliverance from sin. It is unclear whether Jesus saw himself as the Messiah. Some theorize he deliberately avoided calling himself such, perhaps to avoid trouble with the Roman authorities. It was after his death that the idea gained wider acceptance. Although Jesus did not establish Christianity, his teachings and the story of his life and death became the foundation of a new religion that appealed to both Jews and Gentiles in its early years.

The available evidence suggests that the Jew Saul, who became the apostle Paul, played a decisive role in making the story of Jesus the foundation of a new religion powerful enough to sweep over the Mediterranean lands and finally the Western world. Saul renounced Jewish Law because, given his temperament, he felt that his inability to fulfill the Law to the letter made salvation unattainable and left him no choice but to end as a sinner. As a passionate but religiously conflicted Jew, Saul had a vision on the way to Damascus that opened his eyes to a new solution for his inner struggle. Salvation through mere human effort alone being insufficient, one could overcome sin only by divine grace. But this required belief in Jesus Christ, whose divinity was proved by his resurrection.

Saul had grown up to see Jewish Law through the eyes of a

zealous perfectionist. His original zeal for the Law must have concealed a secret resistance against it and a consequent sense of guilt, which at first he relieved by fanatical persecution of Jesus' followers. But how could he persecute others for abandoning the Law when he himself unconsciously longed to do the same? If Jesus was in truth the Messiah, the resurrection inaugurated a new dispensation, a newer Covenant that superseded the old. Those who accepted the divinity of Jesus were freed not only from the old Jewish obligations but from the guilt induced by the neglect of those obligations.

The rebellious self-will that the former Saul struggled against could now be rechanneled into the missionary zeal of the new-born Paul, with his determination to convert both Gentiles and Jews to his newfound source of redemption. The new revelation would make Christianity a worldwide religion, acceptable in a way that Judaism, with its requirement of circumcision and its many legalistic observances, could never hope to become. Now the old Law could finally be replaced by the saving message of Christ.

Christianity adopted the Hebrew scriptures, which it called the Old Testament, and added to them the twenty-seven books of the New Testament. These new books include four Gospels, which recollect the life and sayings of Jesus; a history of the early years of the Church (Acts of the Apostles); letters to early Christian groups (Epistles); and Revelation, which foretells God's intervention in human history at the end of time.

The teachings of Jesus are not represented uniformly in the four Gospels, but they can be summarized generally as follows: to believe in God and to love him, to expect the Kingdom of God (whether on earth or in an afterlife is not always clear), to repent for one's sins, and to love one's neighbor. The Sermon on the Mount, as reported in the Gospel of Matthew (chapters 5–7), is the most famous collection of Jesus' ethical teachings and sayings. It contains the Lord's Prayer, Jesus' version of the Golden Rule, and such famous phrases as "turn the other cheek."

In Christianity, the concept of sin evolved and gained new significance. The Old Testament considered sin to be a violation of God's commandments or rejection of God. To this *actual sin* Christianity added the idea of *original sin*, the doctrine that sinfulness is an inborn condition of all humanity. Original sin then becomes a precondition for Jesus' appearance on earth. The descendants of Adam and Eve are spiritually tainted as a divinely ordained consequence of the act of tasting the forbidden fruit. It was that presumptuous deed which expelled humanity's progenitors from Eden. Heaven was not ready to forgive such insubordinate self-will, even though it was the fallen angel Lucifer in serpent guise who actually persuaded the first couple to defy the divine command. Yet it was their disobedience—the *felix culpa* (fortunate sin), as it came to be called—that made possible humanity's salvation when Jesus was born to redeem the fallen race.

The skeptic cannot help asking: Why did God sacrifice his son to save mankind when he could have done it himself? If Jesus was sacrificed to redeem a sinful humanity, why are we still as sinful as ever? How can faith in the divinity of Jesus be enough to eradicate sin? Why should the indiscretion of Adam and Eve be held against their innocent descendants? Why does Christianity promise salvation out of love for the repentant sinner but prescribe damnation for the honest skeptic?

The Christian account can nevertheless be seen as a symbolic effort to explain humanity's imperfection and offer it hope of redemption. One may disagree with Christian methods of saving the soul but not with the goal of redeeming humanity from its disastrous mode of existence.

Not all Christians take the Gospel story literally. They are nevertheless free to reinterpret it symbolically. Precisely this was done by George Santayana (1863–1952), a philosopher who was born a Catholic and appreciated the poetical aspect of Catholicism but understood its dogmas as symbolic. In *The Idea of Christ in the Gospels*, Santayana subordinates Jesus as a historical person to Christ as a figure whose dual nature symbolizes the complexity of all life. One aspect corresponds to God as objective reality, as the dynamic energy of the world; the other aspect corresponds to spirit, the consciousness that is born to feel and to suffer. Necessarily dependent on the divine energy that generates it, spirit is a finite creation destined for sacrifice on the cross of reality. The experience of living, suffering, and dying enables Christians to identify themselves with Jesus and anticipate reunion with the divine.

For many Christians, the essence of their religion lies less in the belief system and more in the ethics espoused by Jesus in the Gospels. The Jewish emphasis on how life is lived, rather than what one believes, lives on in this tradition. Many activists who are dedicated to working for peace, social justice, and other humanitarian causes draw their inspiration from the teachings and example of Jesus. Recently, certain evangelical Christians have even embraced environmentalism as an expression of their devotion to God's Creation.

According to the Gospel record, the passion of Jesus was a unique event, but in existential terms it symbolizes a universal human predicament. All human beings suffer on the cross of existence. Everyone has to undergo the inevitable ordeals of life and accept the certainty of death. The crucifixion can symbolize the many ways in which human beings renounce the full potentialities of their existence. Even the suffering of anxiety mirrors the suffering on the cross, because in denying an essential part of his own reality, the anxious person in some sense sacrifices his life.

It is significant that the cross projects the human form in its most vulnerable posture, with arms open and front undefended. Those who achieve the self-transcendence symbolized by this posture experience a spiritual resurrection; they have embarked on a path that leads to salvation. Crucifixion and resurrection can therefore be taken to represent any suffering from which a person emerges with greater strength for coping with life.

As a state hospital physician, I treated certain schizophrenics who dramatically realized the redemptive power of Christian faith in their own lives. Convinced at an early age that they could not be true to themselves and still deserve the esteem of others, they felt caught in an insoluble dilemma. The crucifying dilemma of their existence was whether to sacrifice themselves for others or others for themselves. Unable to achieve a resolution, they were reduced to anxiety, rage, and despair. The options available in such a predicament are few, and most are tragic. One is suicide. Another is the paranoid resort to delusional hate and fear. A third is the retreat into the so-called "deterioration" of schizophrenics who have given up trying to maintain even a semblance of normal self-esteem.

Some patients envision the possibility of expiating guilt and restoring their original innocence through identification with the crucified and resurrected Christ. If Jesus could redeem lost souls by his suffering, why can they not redeem themselves by following in his footsteps? Such patients sense that their own lives bear a parallel to the life of Jesus. They too feel despised and rejected. They feel inner potentialities, divine but unlived, that beg to be liberated. Their latent divinity, the capacity to love, has been aborted by lifelong self-contempt. In their search for forgiveness and rebirth, some fall into trance states in which they experience their own crucifixion and resurrection.

I can never forget the time, as a young physician, that I saw a mental hospital patient who lay for three days and nights on the floor of a seclusion room before reawakening in a state of spiritual renewal. Once reborn in this extraordinary fashion, the patient felt free of self-contempt, capable at last of giving and receiving love. His transformation through voluntarily undergoing the Christ ordeal showed him that his own suffering could be a pathway to salvation.

Christian doctrine enables people to fulfill their earthly existence when the full import of its story pervades their living. Jesus dedicated his earthly life to his ideals, then sacrificed his life for a self-transcendent goal. His crucifixion and resurrection can represent any person's achievement of integrity through suffering. Crucifixion symbolizes the suffering that accompanies sacrifice of our personal needs for the sake of others. Resurrection symbolizes the transformation we undergo when we make this sacrifice, enabling us to live up to our unique potential. We gain salvation not through professions of faith but through devoting our finite lives fully to our highest values.

ISLAM

The Arabic word *Islam* can be translated as submission or commitment. The core of Islam is submission to the will of Allah as revealed in the Qur'an. This unique work came to Muhammad (570–632) over many years in trancelike states as a series of directives he ascribed at times to the angel Gabriel and at times directly to Allah. Muhammad saw himself simply as God's messenger, but Muslims honor him as the last and greatest of the prophets. Those who can read the Arabic of the Qur'an have always been struck by the power and eloquence of its language. The translator N. J. Dawood calls it a literary masterpiece and the finest work of classical Arabic prose.

The *surahs*, or numbered sections of the Qur'an, vary in content throughout the course of Muhammad's life. Some offer guidance and warnings to the individual soul; others guide the growing Islamic community. The intuition that led Muhammad to make *submission* the center of Islamic faith shows his awareness that human beings require divine direction in a world they neither comprehend nor control. Allah's paradoxical nature, which embraces omniscience, omnipotence, benevolence, and punitiveness, reflects the unpredictable richness of reality while leaving unsolved the dilemma of determinism versus free will. This is a problem for all theologians, but there is no point in reading the Qur'an as an essay in theology. For Muslims, it is an inspired and immutable set of instructions for living in a world that otherwise has no logical rationale and resists any effort to impose one.

Islamic doctrine, like all monotheistic teachings, reveals a need to bring cosmic unity and divine guidance together in a single frame, to reconcile an earthly reality with a supernal ideal. Parallels with Judaism are worth noting. Both are strict monotheisms, both rely on prophetic revelation, and both have evolved detailed theologico-legal systems for governing society. Each has its rationalistic and mystical dimensions, and each displays the inevitable trends to sectarianism.

The two major Islamic sects, the Sunni and Shia, quarrel to this day, at times to the point of killing each other. They originally disagreed about who was Muhammad's rightful successor, but their competition for political and economic supremacy undoubtedly contributes to their persistent rivalry.

Islamic practice rests on five prescribed "pillars." The first is the *profession of faith*, reciting the twofold creed: there is no god but Allah, and Muhammad is his messenger. Second is the *performance of prayer* at fixed hours five times a day while facing toward Mecca. Third is the *giving of alms*, sharing one's wealth as an act of worship in gratitude for Allah's favor. Fourth is the *duty to fast* as prescribed during the month of Ramadan, a time of spiritual renewal. Fifth is the *Hajj*, or pilgrimage to Mecca, performed if possible at least once in one's lifetime. *Sharia* is the sacred law of Islam and applies to all aspects of life, not just religious practice. The concept of *jihad* (to strive or struggle) can be an internal struggle to live a good Muslim life or an external political or armed struggle to defend Islam. There is no organized priesthood, but special respect is accorded to the descendants of Muhammad and to recognized holy scholars and religious leaders, known as mullahs and ayatollahs.

Islam recognizes numerous prophets, men sent by Allah to deliver his message to the nations at various times in history. Among the prophets mentioned in the Qur'an are well-known figures from the Old and New Testaments, as well as Arabian prophets like Salih, Shu'aib, and of course Muhammad himself. Thus Adam is the first prophet, and Noah, Abraham, Moses, and Jesus are all important prophets in Islam. The Qur'an even recognizes Jesus' virgin birth (Qur'an 3:45–47), although it views Jesus as a human prophet, not the son of God.

A mystical element in Islam, although present in Muhammad himself, was long overshadowed by the rationalistic and intellectual developments of Islamic theology until an emotional need for divine love at last emerged in Sufism. Like the Hasidim of eighteenth-century Judaism, Sufis display the mystic's yearning to escape the confines of the ego into an immediate experience of the divine. Tension between orthodoxy and mysticism has suffused the spiritual life of Muslims with a great range of imaginative responses to the universal longing for unity with the cosmos. Whether self-transcendence implies actual union with Allah or merely a more intense encounter with the divine has been a problem for Islamic theology. The mystic Mansur Al-Hallaj was martyred in the tenth century for allegedly announcing "I am the Truth" and thereby blasphemously identifying himself with God. In striking contrast with Hinduism, which affirms the identity of the Self with the ultimate reality (*Brahman*), orthodox Islam insists on the total and absolute transcendence of Allah.

In medieval times, Islamic civilization attained accomplishments in architecture, in the translation of Greek philosophers, and in medicine, science, and mathematics that far surpassed the European culture of the time. Islamic society also practiced a degree of religious tolerance. In Islamic Spain, Jews could live under a relatively benign regime, unlike during the later Spanish Inquisition.

Today one cannot ignore the intersection of politics and Islam. Perhaps religion is never entirely separate from politics. But traditional Islamic thought in particular tends to reject a distinction between the sacred and the secular, because its aim is to suffuse every facet of life with religious guidance and ideals. Therefore it is not surprising that Islam is deeply divided between older and newer ways of practicing its long and complex tradition. In Algeria, Turkey, and Indonesia, secular and religious parties strive openly for political control. In countries like Iran, whose government is dominated by a conservative religious authority, reformers struggle for influence but suffer political repression. Conversely, Islamic opposition groups such as the Muslim Brotherhood are officially outlawed by the secular governments of countries like Egypt and Syria. Extremist groups complicate the relation of Muslims to one another and the rest of the world. Such extremists resort to such primitive punishments as cutting off a thief's hand for stealing, or flogging—even executing—a woman for infringing on a rigid patriarchal code. Believing that enmity toward Islam justifies any form of violence, they want to supplant secular pluralism with a world order based on their fundamentalist understanding of the Qur'an.

The widespread belief that the Qur'an is the word of God stems from the story of the book's origin and makes it difficult to persuade believers not to interpret it literally. Yet there are moderate and reformist Islamic voices in the Muslim world and in the West. A growing number of Islamic scholars encourage a reinterpretation of the Qur'an in light of contemporary reality. They discourage a literal reading of separate Qur'anic verses and encourage viewing the work as a whole, understanding the historical context from which it sprang, and even admitting the fallibility of Muhammad. The Australian Ameer Ali is one scholar who argues that if the Qur'an is to be a book for all times, it must yield new meanings as times change. He and others attribute the spread of extremist jihadists to a blind faith in the literal interpretation of the Qur'an.

Reinterpretation entails allowing an individual to use his own judgment and innate ethical sense. Strict religious authorities have been notoriously unwilling to permit such autonomy. Independent thinkers are often subject to intimidation by an established clergy who reject any ideas that threaten their supremacy. There have been cases where freethinking Muslims have been condemned to death for insulting Islam. Reformists are freer to speak out in the West, but the call for humane reform is increasingly heard in Muslim nations, especially among educated youth.

RELIGIONS OF THE EAST

In ancient Persia, the prophet Zarathustra (7th–6th century BCE, often latinized as Zoroaster) saw the world locked in a war between the forces of light, led by Ahura Mazda, and the forces of darkness, led by Ahriman. Ahura Mazda, the beneficent creator and judge, embodied truth, light, and life. His evil opponent Ahriman was the destructive spirit, embodying lies, darkness, and death. Both gods and men were thought to have the freedom to choose between good and evil. The cosmic struggle was to culminate in a final judgment at the end of time, ushering in a new world where good would prevail. Belief in the supremacy of Ahura Mazda began to supplant the polytheism of early Persia and set the stage for the monotheisms of Judaism, Christianity, and Islam. But the dualistic framework of Zoroastrianism (good versus evil) persists as an important theme in modern religious thought. The conquest of Persia by an Islamic empire in the seventh century forced the followers of Zarathustra, later known as Parsis, to flee to India, where they form a small minority.

The Far East developed many forms of religious life that are worthy of attention, but despite their interest and variety, we will limit ourselves here to Hinduism, Taoism, and Buddhism. Hinduism and Buddhism, along with Jainism and Sikhism, are known as the *Dharmic* religions, as opposed to the *Abrahamic* religions of the West (Judaism, Christianity, Islam). The Sanskrit word *dharma*, derived from the root "established" or "firm," is used in various ways. It can mean the universal law or principle of cosmic and individual existence, but it can also refer to law in the sense of specific religious doctrine. In this tradition, an individual aims to live in accord with the essential nature of the universe and his relation to it.

Hinduism is probably the world's oldest living religion. Hindus think of it as not just a religion but a way of life, since religious experience takes precedence over religious doctrine. The *Vedas* are the sacred scriptures of the Hindus, the oldest of which, the Rig Veda, probably dates back to 1200 BCE. The *Vedas* (*Veda* means "knowledge") are thought not to have originated with either man or God, but to have been always present as eternal truth. They were "heard" by inspired ancient sages who then recorded them in the Sanskrit language.

Hinduism was originally a luxuriant polytheism. But in such later writings as the Upanishads and the Bhagavad Gita, Hindu sages came to view these multiple deities as the various appearances of a single impersonal God or *Brahman* (the ultimate reality) which is all-encompassing and beyond description. According to the Hindu sages, the world as it appears to us with its countless diverse phenomena is an illusion (*maya*), not in the sense that it has no reality, but that its familiar aspect is not the final or total reality.

The individual body is a perishable and therefore illusory entity. Only the soul (*Atman*) is real, and it is part of the ultimate divine reality (*Brahman*), as articulated in the Upanishad formula *Tat tvam asi* (Thou art that). In a common analogy, the individual soul is as a single drop of water in an infinite ocean of eternal consciousness. Thus unity and plurality are reconciled. The *Atman* survives death and is reincarnated in a new life. The cycle of birth and death (*samsara*) proceeds according to the principle of cause and effect (*karma*, literally "act"), whereby an individual's actions determine his circumstances in his next life. Liberation from *samsara* occurs when an individual realizes the truth that *Atman* and *Brahman* are one.

While the Western monotheisms understand God as a single power that transcends the world and its creatures, Hinduism views all manifestations of existence as a cosmic unity, and it therefore accepts a variety of beliefs and practices without insisting that only one is correct. Another expression of the pluralism in Hinduism, however, is the social stratification of Indian society. The Rig Veda describes four social classes that form the basis of the caste system. While it is impossible to know whether the religion determined this reality or merely reflected it, it must be said that Hindu society accepted the inequity along with the diversity of this social hierarchy.

In China, the philosophy or religion known as Taoism coexisted with Confucianism from ancient times, and ultimately contributed to later developments in Buddhism. Taoism teaches that living in accordance with the Tao (the Way, the natural flow of the universe) is the only sane mode of existence. The formless Tao, encompassing both being and not-being, animates everything. It is the source and goal of all that exists. Natural phenomena are in a constant state of flux, as are human perceptions. The opposing but complementary forces of Yin and Yang (sometimes too narrowly defined as female and male or darkness and light) are not completely distinct or mutually exclusive, but are mutually supportive and even transformable into one another. In the same way, good and evil are ultimately indistinguishable because they too are not mutually exclusive; they tend to shift and evolve into each other, as day evolves into night.

It is impossible to name or understand reality because its complex and fluctuating character cannot be reduced to our limiting concepts. The sage therefore clears his mind of obstructing thoughts so that the Tao can work through him. The principle of *wei wu wei* (literally *do not-do*) counsels not *in*action, but action that does not disrupt the intrinsic flow and movement of existence. Humanity's basic error is the futile ambition to impose our will on a reality that we are inherently unable to comprehend or control.

The most widely known Taoist text is the *Tao Tê Ching* (The Book of the Way and its Virtue), the frequently cryptic and paradoxical treatise attributed to the Chinese philosopher Lao Tzu. While the *Tao Tê Ching* offers its sage advice to rulers, the often witty parables of Chuang Tzu speak about matters of ordinary life. In one famous story, Chuang Tzu dreams he is a butterfly, then awakes to wonder whether he is Chuang Tzu dreaming he is a butterfly or a butterfly dreaming he is Chuang Tzu. He uses this simple story to demonstrate the continual interrelation and transformation of things.

Buddhism has its roots in Hinduism but also shares important features with Taoism. Buddhism is a nontheistic religion or practical philosophy, in some ways even a form of psychology. Like Hinduism, it is not just a set of beliefs but a way of life. Its teachings aim to guide a person to an enlightened existence. Like Taoism, Buddhism sees existence as forever in flux. Like Hinduism, it teaches that man suffers from ignorance or illusion about the nature of his existence. Buddhism shares Hinduism's concept of *samsara*, but it rejects the idea of caste. Buddhism also rejects the idea of an eternal soul (*Atman*) or ultimate reality (*Brahman*), arguing that both are transitory and illusory. The individual is an ever changing consciousness in an ephemeral body, no more permanent than the clouds in the sky.

The founder of Buddhism, Siddhartha Gautama (563–483 CE), taught that all human suffering stems from the illusion of selfhood, which leads to desire or craving. Since both the self and what is desired are continuously evolving into something new, any attachment to a particular state ends in frustration and disappointment. One can liberate oneself from the pattern of desire and suffering by following the right path in thought, speech, action, mindfulness, and meditation. The aim is to awaken from illusion, which liberates one from *samara*, the endless cycle of birth, suffering, death, and rebirth. A person who has achieved this awakening is called a buddha (enlightened). The term *nirvana* refers to the state of liberation or enlightenment, not a place in an afterlife but a spiritual goal that can be experienced in this present existence.

Buddhist doctrine is more a method than a belief. It is a *yana*, a ferry from the shore of illusion to the shore of enlightenment. To practice Buddhism is to embark on this voyage. Once a passenger has reached the other shore, the ferry is no longer needed and is left behind. Therefore an enlightened one no longer bothers to distinguish between *nirvana* and *samsara* because he lives with *tathata* (suchness), a direct experience of reality without the need for intermediating concepts.

The Japanese developed a unique and audacious form of Buddhism called Zen. It flowered when Buddhist seeds were transplanted from India to China, where Buddhism mingled with Taoism and then moved on to Japanese soil. Bodhidharma, the first Zen patriarch, repudiated all sermons and texts. He enlightened his disciples with austere directness by frustrating their every attempt to substitute verbal doctrine for authentic experience. For example, if a student should ask, "What is the secret of Zen?" the master might reply not by answering the question but by asking another question, for example, "What are the original features that you have before you are born?" The disciple must wrestle with such arcane *koans* (paradoxical riddles) until *satori* (sudden intuitive enlightenment) shatters his habitual modes of thinking.

In summary, Eastern wisdom invites us to recognize our true nature, to ignore our imagined importance or unimportance, and to accept our transitory role in the cosmic flux. To live in this fashion is to transcend self-centeredness and become one with the universe—or to put it in other words, we have attained what is sometimes called salvation.

MYSTICISM

The union of the individual with the universe or the divine, while an essential part of the Eastern (*Dharmic*) religions, has been less central in the Western (*Abrahamic*) religions. The sacrament of the Eucharist in the Catholic mass comes closest to representing such a union, since an individual receives or incorporates Christ into his life through the taking of wafer and wine. But within each of the Abrahamic religions one can find a mystical current that echoes the *Dharmic* religions' identification of the individual with the divine. The mystical experience can be equally described as a direct intuition, a way of knowing, or a state of consciousness in which the individual feels at one with what may be termed God, the Divine, or Ultimate Reality (*Brahman*).

Jesus said, "He that loseth his life for my sake shall find it" (Matthew 10:39). In the same vein, Juan de la Cruz wrote, "Muero porque no muero" (I die because I do not die). An Islamic Sufi saying expresses the same idea, "Die before you die." The paradoxical nature of such statements stems from their attempt to address a reality that lies outside the bounds of ordinary language or logic. The idea is that the "death" or dissolving of individual consciousness is necessary for the individual's merging with the greater "life" of an all-encompassing spirit. This death is not necessarily a physical death; it is a living experience of transcending the self. This can happen in real moments of time, but it is experienced as timeless. Such apparent contradictions, like Zen *koans*, ask us to break out of our habitual modes of awareness, to realize we are not finite or separate from the universe but part of something infinite. And because we cannot conceive the infinite, the mystical experience is not conceptual but intuitive and direct.

It may be helpful to read how a mystic describes his own experience. The Indian poet Rabindranath Tagore reported to a friend:

> As I was watching it, suddenly, in a moment, a veil seemed to be lifted from my eyes. I found the world wrapt in an inexpressible glory with its waves of joy and beauty bursting and breaking on all

sides. The thick cloud of sorrow that lay on my heart was pierced through and through by the light of the world, which was everywhere radiant. . . .

There was nothing and no one whom I did not love at that moment. . . . I stood on the veranda and watched the coolies as they tramped down the road. Their movements, their forms, their countenances seemed strangely wonderful to me, as if they were all moving like waves in the great ocean of the world. When one young man placed his hand on the shoulder of another and passed laughingly by, it was a remarkable event to me. . . . I seemed to witness, in the wholeness of my vision, the movements of the body of all humanity, and to feel the beat of the music and the rhythms of a mystic dance.

Letters to a Friend

The French philosopher Simone Weil was born Jewish, raised agnostic, and later attracted to Catholicism. Here is her description of a mystical experience:

It was during one of these recitations that, as I told you, Christ himself came down and took possession of me.

In my arguments about the insolubility of the problem of God I had never foreseen the possibility of that, of a real contact, person to person, here below, between a human being and God. I had vaguely heard tell of things of this kind, but I had never believed in them. In the *Fioretti* the accounts of apparitions rather put me off if anything, like the miracles in the Gospels. Moreover, in this sudden possession of me by Christ, neither my senses nor my imagination had any part; I only felt in the midst of my suffering the presence of a love, like that which one can read in the smile of a beloved face. . . . God in his mercy had prevented me from reading the mystics, so that it should be evident to me that I had not invented this absolutely unexpected contact.

Yet I still half refused, not my love but my intelligence. For it seemed to me certain, and I still think so today, that one cannot wrestle enough with God if one does it out of pure regard for truth.

Christ likes us to prefer truth to him, because, being Christ, he is truth. If one turns aside from him to go toward truth, one will not go far before falling into his arms.

Waiting for God

Note the emphasis on love in both of these accounts. The essence of divinity is experienced as loving, not as judging or punishing. The statement "God is love" can sound to a skeptic like a simplistic cliché, but it may be a sincere but inadequate attempt to express a mystical insight in words. In the symbolic language of some mystical traditions, ecstatic longing for God may be expressed in erotic metaphors. The Christian notion of the Church as the Bride of Christ uses marriage as a symbol of union with God. The tenth-century Islamic mystic Mansur Al-Hallaj wrote, "I have become the One I love, and the One I love has become me! We are two spirits infused in a (single) body" (Louis Massignon, *The Passion of al-Hallaj*).

Mystical states are ineffable, unintelligible to those who have not experienced them. Yet they are a form of knowledge, marked by insight into a level of truth that is unavailable to analytical intelligence. The mystic often resorts to metaphors or symbolic language in trying to explain this exceptional reality. The twelfth-century Sufi mystic Abu Hamid Al-Ghazali wrote about the inadequacy of language in his book *Deliverance from Error*: "[Mystics] come to stages in the 'way' which it is hard to describe in language; if a man attempts to express these, his words inevitably contain what is erroneous."

Symbols may be helpful to those who attempt to describe mystical experience, but symbols are no substitute for the experience itself. Flannery O'Connor, a writer and devout Catholic, once wrote about a conversation in which the Holy Ghost was described as a symbol:

I then said, in a very shaky voice, "Well, if it's a symbol, to hell with it." That was all the defense I was capable of but I realize now that this is all I will ever be able to say about it, outside of a story, except that it is the center of existence for me; all the rest of life is expendable.

The Habit of Being

To this profoundly religious woman, it must have been inconceivable (hence the shaky voice) to reduce her experience to the level of symbolism. A symbol stands for something other than itself. If O'Connor experienced the Holy Ghost as the center of her existence, it was a reality to be lived, not a symbol to be interpreted. Explaining how integral religion was to her life, she wrote, "I feel that if I were not a Catholic, I would have no reason to write, no reason to see, no reason ever to feel horrified or even to enjoy anything."

Mystical experience can take many forms—a sensation, realization, vision, revelation, or dream—but it always affects the entire person, not just the mind. Sometimes the experience comes uninvited. The Prophet Muhammad reportedly had no thought of receiving divine messages and at first did not know what to make of them. Various traditions have nevertheless developed ways to invite the experience or at least make a person receptive to its possibility. Hindus and Buddhists use meditation and yoga to train the mind and body. Meditation and prayer are used in the West as well. Zen masters use *koans* to frustrate reason and prod their disciples into sudden enlightenment. Hasidic Jews and Sufi Muslims transcend language and intellect by singing and dancing their way to an ecstatic state. Ascetics in the East and West use fasting, personal isolation, and other kinds of self-denial to alter their consciousness.

Like the existence of God, the validity of one's mystical experience is beyond proof. To a skeptic, it is merely a subjective experience. To orthodox religious hierarchy, it often represents heresy. A mystic is less concerned with questions of dogma or such distinctions as *subjective* versus *objective*. The inadequacy of verbal descriptions or explanations does nothing to diminish the import of the mystical experience for the one who undergoes it.

ATHEISM

Religious experience does not require belief in God or a hereafter. A skeptic can appreciate and enjoy religious literature and ritual without such belief. He can also react with a sense of awe to the mysteries of the universe. But until demonstrable evidence confirms the existence of God, an atheist or agnostic is justified in maintaining a skeptical attitude. The fact that most human beings affirm a belief in God and feel a need to worship him does not prove his reality. Humanity's many and varied concepts of God shed no credible light on either his nature or his existence.

Contrary to popular myth, atheists are no worse than the rest of the human race. They are at times condemned as evil and dangerous. The implication is that they condone immorality and that goodness is impossible without godliness. Despite the stigma, there is no evidence that atheists are less ethical than their God-fearing brethren. Such prejudice merely indicates a widespread suspicion of nonconformity and a reluctance to turn to reason when deeply ingrained beliefs are in question.

Believers, atheists, and agnostics all face the same existential questions. Then why do they differ? Skeptics can tolerate the absence of convincing answers. Believers who rely on faith feel no need of proof. Atheists and agnostics would rather live with uncertainty than believe what is unprovable. The great physicist Albert Einstein affirmed his religious sensibility while denying a belief in the supernatural: "I am a deeply religious nonbeliever. . . . This is a somewhat new kind of religion" (letter to Hans Mühsam, 1954).

A NOTE ON
THE AESTHETIC

Even with all our failures and contradictions, we cannot be denied our redeeming features. If not for love, friendship, and the unique role of aesthetic fulfillment, existence would be an arid exercise. The capacity for aesthetic experience enables us to tolerate aspects of life that would otherwise be intolerable. Aesthetic enjoyment is as vital as food or drink or sex.

What would life be without the music of Bach and Mozart, the poetry of Homer and Dante, the plays of Shakespeare and novels of Dostoevsky, the art of Michelangelo and Picasso, the philosophies of Plato, Spinoza, and Santayana, or the religious insights of the scriptures and the Talmud? Such creativity offers an unsurpassable education in art and thought. Darwin and Einstein belong in a comparable list of scientists. Mathematics is exceptional in its power to yield aesthetic pleasure and intellectual satisfaction at the very same moment. Mathematicians from Euclid to Gauss must not be omitted from our list of creative minds.

The human beings who think and create on this level no doubt have their personal shortcomings, but their work stands apart from our senseless conflicts and contributes to building what could be a civilization in fact, not merely in name. Granted that aesthetic perfection is not enough to save us from the disasters we inflict on ourselves, it might be enough to justify preserving our paradoxical human species.

WHERE ARE
WE HEADED?

A fundamental question hangs over us like a sword of Damocles. Do we desire—are we even able—to free ourselves from the misunderstanding and distrust that have made human life a tragicomedy? The present state of the world calls for a drastic reassessment of what we have been calling civilization. Without a searching reappraisal, there is no hope of remaking a self-defeating civilization that celebrates war, fosters misunderstanding, and frustrates human fulfillment.

Being human comes with a price. Given our conflicts, our inadequate communication, and the contradictions between our rational potential and our irrational nature, there is more than enough to account for our quandary as a species. We reinforce the paradoxical character of human life by thoughtlessly misusing our capabilities or failing to apply them. At times, the power of communication imparts useful knowledge; at other times it deceives and misleads. Mutual understanding is constantly vulnerable to the unreconciled diversity of human language and human purposes. The need to live with one another produces everything between the extremes of love and hate, or war and peace. So long as we disregard our shared humanity and emphasize our differences, we continue to risk self-destruction.

157

We have always maintained this system by our disregard of reason. We have hardly begun to reconcile our insistent but divisive goals. Why do we make power a higher priority than peace? Will we ever share the finite resources of the earth with all who are in need? Erich Kahler's assessment was correct: "We stand at the crossroad between the annihilation of the West and the unification of humanity" (*The Meaning of History*).

A rational response will not be easy for a human race that prefers to evade whatever it finds disturbing. The specific social and interpersonal difficulties reviewed in this book all demonstrate our defensive retreat from reality. This retreat is conspicuous, for example, in the anxiety that results from denying motives one has learned not to acknowledge. A similar retreat is apparent in all mental disorder that is marked by impaired judgment about oneself and the world. We understand ourselves only so far as we know what we want and what we are trying to do. Clarity on these points is the goal of psychological insight, but has implications far beyond the life of the individual. Never having fully understood our world or our own nature, we have repeatedly come up with incomplete conceptions of both. Our most valuable insights arise from a level deeper than conscious intelligence. While consciousness plays a unique and indispensable role in life, it is an equivocal gift, for the anomalies of existence outstrip our powers of conscious analysis.

The scientific understanding of ourselves and world may be the most successful so far, but even this version has its limits. Neither science nor technology can provide our necessary direction, because those who engage in these enterprises are handicapped by their own human shortcomings. Well-meaning philosophers have offered their wisdom for centuries, but how far have they actually advanced civilization?

Religious belief in some form has always been a predictable response to the quandaries of existence, but it has also ignored or distorted certain aspects of reality. People may be deeply religious without comprehending the implications of their own faith, let alone the faiths of others. They are thus unlikely to see what has been evident to such thinkers as Spinoza and Santayana, who realized that much traditional religion is mythical or symbolic and need not be taken literally. This is not to deny that metaphorical language may be creatively insightful, for its power of poetic illumination can rise to the level of profound art. When the language of religion reaches that height, it helps reconcile us to an enigmatic world. But with all their insights, historical religions have not provided convincing solutions for the world as a whole.

One helpful insight that religious minds continue to rediscover is the need to affirm our worth without losing our humility. This balanced self-awareness helps us recognize our proper place in the world and enables respectful communication with our adversaries. Christians can learn both humility and self-worth from Christ's all-embracing love. Jews are taught by the Hasidic Rabbi Simcha Bunam (1765–1827) that they need two pockets: one for the words "For my sake was the world created" (Mishnah, Sanhedrin 4.5), and one for "I am but dust and ashes" (Genesis 18:27).

Is salvation in any form possible for paradoxical beings like us? In Shakespeare's *King Lear*, the ill-starred Earl of Gloucester concludes there is no purpose to our existence:

> As flies to wanton boys are we to the gods;
> They kill us for their sport.

Not all of us are ready to accept this embittered version of life. Nature has implanted in us too deep and instinctive a faith in life's promise for us to surrender hope prematurely. Perhaps we can still transform our ordeal into a life worth living. But if we are destined to be sacrificial victims of this world, we have no choice but to endure the ordeal. In his Spartan view of life as a contest that one cannot win, the poet Rilke asks, "Who speaks of victory? To endure is everything." Perhaps a modicum of salvation occurs in those exceptional moments when delight in an incredible universe helps us transcend its indifference to what becomes of us. But moments of subjective fulfillment cannot alter the destiny of a world that is neither consistent nor rational.

The best we can do is be true to ourselves in the face of every opposing force. To actualize existence with every available resource is to live, in the words of the Talmud, for the sake of heaven. The Deuteronomist tells us to love God with all our heart, with all our soul, and with all our might. Everyone is born with a natural drive to assert one's will, but sooner or later that will must redirect itself to facing— and accepting—all reality. Two thousand years ago, Rabbi Hillel summoned us to live in that spirit when he asked:

> If I am not for myself, who will be for me?
> If I am for myself alone, what am I?
> And if not now, when?
> Mishnah, Pirkei Avot 1.3 (Sayings of the Fathers)

In the end, every thoughtful person recognizes the urgency of changing course while there still is time. A character in H. G. Wells' *The Croquet Player*, when he begins to realize what the world has come to, proclaims, "Only giants can save the world from complete relapse and so we—who care for civilization—have to become giants." He goes on, "There will be no choice before a human being but to be either a driven animal or a stern devotee to that true civilization, that disciplined civilization, that has never yet been achieved." These words were written in the last century, but since then the world situation has continued to change for the worse.

Whoever predicts what no one wants to hear can look forward to the fate of Cassandra, whose prophetic warnings were always ignored. Yet the future is never predictable with complete certainty. We dare not give up.

ENVOI

Be cheerful, sir,
Our revels now are ended. These our actors,
As I foretold you, were all spirits, and
Are melted into air, into thin air:
And, like the baseless fabric of this vision,
The cloud-capp'd towers, the gorgeous palaces,
The solemn temples, the great globe itself,
Yea, all which it inherit, shall dissolve,
And, like this insubstantial pageant faded,
Leave not a rack behind. We are such stuff
As dreams are made on; and our little life
Is rounded with a sleep.

Shakespeare, *The Tempest*

BIBLIOGRAPHY

Adler, Alfred. *Social Interest: A Challenge to Mankind*. London: Faber & Faber, 1943.

Andreasen, Nancy C., and Donald W. Black. *An Introductory Textbook of Psychiatry*, 4th ed. Arlington, VA: American Psychiatric Publishing, 2006.

Angyal, Andras. *Foundations for a Science of Personality*. New York: Commonwealth Fund, 1941.

Ansbacher, Heinz, and Rowena Ansbacher. *The Individual Psychology of Alfred Adler*. New York: Basic Books, 1956.

Aristotle. *On the Soul*, translated by W. S. Hett. Loeb Classical Library. Cambridge, MA: Harvard University Press, 2000.

Arnold, Matthew. "The Study of Poetry." In *Essays in Criticism*. New York: Everyman's Library/Dutton, 1966.

Benoît, Hubert. *The Supreme Doctrine: Psychological Studies in Zen Thought*. New York: Viking, 1955.

Bloom, Harold. *Jesus and Yahweh: The Names Divine*. New York: Grove, 1990.

Bunge, Mario. *Causality: The Place of the Causal Principle in Modern Science*, 3rd rev. ed. New York: Dover, 1979.

Chuang Tzu. *The Complete Works of Chuang Tzu*. Translated by Burton Watson. New York and London: Columbia University Press, 1964 and 1996.

Cicero, Marcus Tullius. *De Finibus*, translated by H. Rackham. Loeb Classical Library. Cambridge, MA: Harvard University Press, 1989.

Crick, Francis. *The Astonishing Hypothesis: The Scientific Search for the Soul*. New York: Scribner, 1994.

Davies, Paul. *The Cosmic Blueprint: New Discoveries in Nature's Creative Ability to Order the Universe*. New York: Simon and Schuster, 1988.

———. *The Mind of God: The Scientific Basis for a Rational World*. New York: Simon and Schuster, 1992.

Dawood, N. J., trans. *The Koran*. London: Penguin, 2004.

Diamond, Jared. *Guns, Germs, and Steel: The Fates of Human Societies*. New York: Norton, 2005.

Dow, David R. *Executed on a Technicality: Lethal Injustice on America's Death Row*. Boston: Beacon Press, 2005.

Dreikurs, Rudolph. "The Adlerian Approach to Psychodynamics." In *Contemporary Psychotherapies*, edited by M. I. Stein. New York: Free Press, 1961.

Einstein, Albert. *Albert Einstein, The Human Side: New Glimpses from His Archives*, edited by Banesh Hoffman and Helen Dukas. Princeton, NJ: Princeton University Press, 1981.

———. *The New Quotable Einstein*, collected and edited by Alice Calaprice. Princeton, NJ: Princeton University Press, 2005.

Eliade, Mircea. *The Sacred and the Profane: The Nature of Religion*. Translated by Willard R. Trask. New York: Harcourt Brace, 1959.

Freud, Sigmund. *Civilization and Its Discontents*, translated by James Strachey. New York: Norton, 1989.

Friends Committee on National Legislation. http://www.fcnl.org.

Ghazali, Abu Hamid Muhammad al-. *The Faith and Practice of Al-Ghazali*, translated by W. Montgomery Watt. Oxford: Oneworld Publications, 1995. First published 1982 by Kazi Publications.

Gilbert, Gustave Mark. *Nuremberg Diary*. New York: Da Capo Press, 1995.

Happold, F. C. *Mysticism: A Study and an Anthology*, 3rd ed. London: Penguin, 1991.

Hedges, Chris. *War Is a Force That Gives Us Meaning*. New York: Public Affairs, 2002.

Hick, John. *An Interpretation of Religion: Human Responses to the Transcendent*, 2nd ed. New Haven, CT: Yale University Press, 2004.

Horney, Karen. *Neurosis and Human Growth*. New York: Norton, 1950.

John of the Cross, Saint. *The Poems of St. John of the Cross*, translated by Ken Krabbenhoft. New York: Harcourt, 1999.

Jung, C. G. *The Archetypes and the Collective Unconscious: The Collected Works of C. G. Jung*, edited by Gerhard Adler, translated by R. F. C. Hull. Bollingen Series 20. Princeton, NJ: Princeton University Press, 1981.

Kafka, Franz. "Reflections on Sin, Pain, Hope, and the True Way," *Dearest Father, Stories and Other Writings*, translated by Ernst Kaiser and Eithne Wilkins. New York: Schocken, 1954.

Kahler, Erich. *The Meaning of History*. New York: Braziller, 1964.

Kapleau, Philip. *The Three Pillars of Zen*. New York: Doubleday, 1989.

Kerbaj, Richard. "Prophet Not Perfect, Says Islamic Scholar." *Australian*, October 4, 2006.

Kohut, Heinz. *How Does Analysis Cure?* Chicago: University of Chicago Press, 1984.

Kovitz, Benjamin. "Letter to a Beginning Psychotherapist." *American Journal of Psychotherapy* 52, no. 1 (Winter 1998).

———. "On the Sinner in the Saint: A Psychological Note on Teresa of Avila." In *Centenary of St. Teresa*. Carmelite Studies 3. Washington, DC: Institute of Carmelite Studies, 1984.

———. "The Psychiatrist Interrogated." In *The Future of Psychotherapy*. International Psychiatry Clinics 6, no. 3. Boston: Little, Brown, 1969.

Lao Tzu. *Tao Te Ching*, translated by D. C. Lau. New York: Knopf, 1982 and 1989.

Lundberg, Ferdinand. *The Natural Depravity of Mankind: Observations on the Human Condition*. New York: Barricade Books, 1994.

MacIntyre, Alasdair C. *After Virtue: A Study in Moral Theory*, 2nd ed. Notre Dame, IN: University of Notre Dame Press, 1984.

MacLean, Paul D. *The Triune Brain in Evolution: Role in Paleocerebral Functions*. New York: Plenum Press, 1990.

Maimonides, Moses. *Guide of the Perplexed*, translated by Shlomo Pines. Chicago: University of Chicago Press, 1963.

Massingnon, Louis. *The Passion of al-Hallaj: Mystic and Martyr of Islam*, translated by Herbert Mason. Princeton, NJ: Princeton University Press, 1982.

Mead, George H. *Mind, Self and Society*. Chicago: University of Chicago Press, 1934.

National Priorities Organization. http://nationalpriorities.org.

O'Connor, Flannery. *The Habit of Being: Letters of Flannery O'Connor.* New York: Farrar, Straus and Giroux, 1979.

Ortega y Gasset, José. "In Search of Goethe from Within." In *The Dehumaniza-tion of Art and Other Essays on Art, Culture, and Literature*, rev. ed., translated by Willard R. Trask. Princeton, NJ: Princeton University Press, 1968.

———. *On Love: Aspects of a Single Theme*, translated by Toby Talbot. New York: Greenwich Editions/Meridian Books, 1957.

Osler, William. *The Principles and Practice of Medicine*, 23rd ed. New York: Appleton and Lange, 1996.

Otto, Rudolf. *The Idea of the Holy: An Inquiry into the Non-Rational Factor in the Idea of the Divine and Its Relation to the Rational*, 2nd ed., translated by John W. Harvey. New York: Oxford University Press, 1958.

Polanyi, Michael. *Personal Knowledge: Towards a Post-Critical Philosophy.* Chicago: University of Chicago Press, 1962.

Saffo, Mary Beth. "Accidental Elegance." *American Scholar* 74 (2005).

Santayana, George. *The Idea of Christ in the Gospels; or, God in Man: A Critical Essay.* New York: Scribner, 1946.

———. *The Life of Reason; or, The Phases of Human Progress.* New York: Scribner, 1954.

———. *Realms of Being.* New York: Cooper Square, 1972.

———. *Soliloquies in England and Later Soliloquies.* New York: Scribner, 1922.

Sheffer, Susannah, and Renny Cushing. *Creating More Victims: How Execu-tions Hurt the Families Left Behind.* Cambridge, MA: Murder Victims' Families for Human Rights, 2006. http://www.willsworld.com/~mvfhr/.

Skinner, B. F. *Recent Issues in the Analysis of Behavior.* Columbus, OH: Merrill, 1989.

Smith, Huston. *Why Religion Matters: The Fate of the Human Spirit in an Age of Disbelief.* San Francisco: Harper and Row, 2001.

Spinoza, Benedict de. *Ethics including the Improvement of the Under-standing*, translated by R. H. M. Elwes. Amherst, NY: Prometheus Books, 1989.

Spong, John Shelby. *Rescuing the Bible from Fundamentalism: A Bishop Rethinks the Meaning of Scripture.* San Francisco: Harper, 1992.

Sullivan, Harry Stack. *The Collected Works of Harry Stack Sullivan.* New York: Norton, 1953–1956.

Szasz, Thomas S. *The Myth of Mental Illness*. New York: Hoeber, 1961.

Tagore, Rabindranath. *Letters to a Friend*, edited by C. F. Andrews. New York: Macmillan, 1930.

Teresa of Avila, Saint. *The Life of Teresa of Jesus: The Autobiography of Teresa of Avila*, translated and edited by E. Allison Peers. Garden City, NY: Image Books, 1960.

Weil, Simone. *Waiting for God*, translated by Emma Craufurd. New York: Harper and Row, 1973. First published 1951 by Putnam.

Wells, H. G. *The Croquet Player*. New York: Viking, 1937.

———. *The Outline of History*. New York: Doubleday, 1940.

Yalom, Irvin D. *Existential Psychotherapy*. New York: Basic Books, 1980.

Zinn, Howard. "The Uses of History and the War on Terrorism." *Progressive* 70, no. 11 (November 2006). http.progressive.org.